9 8 7 6 5 4 3 2 1 0
First published 2021

Bible references are from a wide range of translations.

ISBN 978-1-9161729-5-1

All enquires to theweddedhare@gmail.com

Cover design and Typesetting by Angela Selfe
Cover background image by www.freepik.com

Printed in the UK

UNCHARTED

Navigating the emerging era

HALLMARKS & HINTS

Jonathan Bugden

Published by
spirit level communications

Contents

A new epoch 7

We have not been this way before 9

Introduction 10

1. Enjoying the unknown 18
2. Heaven's perspective 20
3. A healthier spirit 22
4. Embracing mystery over certitude 26
5. Leaving the status quo to find adventure 28
6. Encounter and experience more than knowledge 30
7. Destiny is much more than opportunity 32
8. God's rhythm 34
9. Courage subduing fear, and coping replaced by conquering 38
10. Sonship liberates the orphan 40
11. Displacement of shame and low self-esteem 42
12. Peace in storms 44
13. From performance to radiance 46
14. Intimacy replaces formality 48
15. Custodians of creation 50
16. Integrity 52

17. Creativity 54

18. Lovers not consumers 56

19. Humility 58

20. Honour displaces judgement 60

21. Revelation supersedes information 62

22. Prayer redefined 64

23. Persecution 66

24. Generosity 68

25. Contentment not comparison 70

26. Fruit matters more than gifting; maturity redefined 72

27. Fragility and resilience 74

28. Knowledge and Wisdom 78

29. From prophetic words to fulfilment 80

30. An eternal perspective 82

31. A motivation to contribute rather than acquire 84

32. Outrageous love and the ministry of reconciliation 88

Author's note 91

33. The surrender of control to focus on empowerment 92

34. Institution to fluid community 96

35. Family not hierarchy 98

36. Governance in the new era 102

37. Purpose before programme 106

38. Gardeners instead of Builders 108
39. Big is no longer best 110
40. Encounters not lectures 112
41. Ambassadors replace Recruiters 114
42. Religion is the enemy! 116
43. Oneness that is real 118
44. Deconstruction 120
45. A love revolution 122

Words to the 'wise'

Permission is granted . . . 127
See and hear clearly 128
Recalibration is required 129
Don't be confused – see clearly 131
Bask in intimacy with God 132
Change of specification 134
Fear Fighters 135
Get used to different 137
Entwined with the Three 138
Divergence 139
Perception 140

My journal 141

A new epoch

The arrival of Jesus on earth heralded a new epoch in history.

We are, I believe, being called to transition into yet another new age.

When a new era arrives, only a few people are aware of it – they are those who are wired and called to be the **early pioneers**. It is this small group who start to carve out a new path on previously untouched land.

This creates a visible path for others (the main body of **pioneers**) to pick out, and it is then this group who (due to their numbers, giftings, and skills) create a more obvious route for the next group (**early 'settlers'**) to walk.

The combined journey of all these groups creates a roadway that is secure, tested, and safe enough for the rest (**settlers and late settlers**) to travel on should they choose to. Often people who are pioneers think it's just them who are walking this weird, puzzling new road; but in fact, they are creating a path for others to follow.

If you don't seem to have a path ahead then it may well be that you are creating a new one!

Explorers and discoverers, by very definition, go into uncharted territory.

It's so helpful to know which one of these people groups you are part of. Pioneers are both misunderstood by and annoying to settlers.

Settlers, on the other hand, are incredibly frustrating to pioneers.

Understand and honour those in other groups.

It is not about pigeon-holing ourselves or others but about understanding where strengths and weaknesses lie.

Under the tutelage of Holy Spirit, adopt a posture and attitude that will allow you to think original thoughts.

From a heart that longs to go deeper and swim in the endless ocean of intimacy with Jesus, be secure in yourself and in God to enable you to ask previously unasked questions.

Be reckless in your trust in God and your love of others and covenant with God to take great leaps of faith.

Be brave and follow your spirit's prompting. Boldly and humbly follow our invisible companion and guide when He whispers, "This is the way", especially as we 'have not walked this way before'.

We are all novices on this new path – there are no experts (especially true for those who were 'experts' in the previous era).

New really does mean New!

Prayer/Declaration

Lord, I want to be humble, teachable, and yielded to You.
Holy Spirit, I am ready to receive the revelation and realignment from heaven that is waiting for me.
I discard my own agenda to collaborate with yours, God.
Release to me the discernment to 'know' the times.
There is no one else like You – what an honour to know You!

We have not been this way before

I am totally persuaded that we are living in a 'Kairos' moment where everything, including the Church of Jesus, is passing through a portal that starts the journey into a radically different environment on multiple levels.

It's hard to overstate the magnitude and intensity of this mega transition!

This journey inexorably requires our willingness to re-examine our foundational belief system under the guidance of the Holy Spirit.

The level of upheaval and shaking during this time is reminiscent of the disturbance and disruption that Jesus caused when he lived on earth. He offended the religious, broke rules, and appeared to arrogantly go against the teaching and practices of those who served and represented God.

As a result of this God-initiated transition, much of who we thought we were and what we did is no longer fit for current purpose.

It's not that what went before was bad but that it is now inadequate.

God is extracting His Church from its religious, prison-like context.

We can only move forward with relational connection and an authentic reality that is spirit based and Spirit led.

May you so know the love and affirmation of God that it enables you to travel over this history-defining threshold.

Introduction

Questions that are usually asked on a journey of transition:

What do we do now?
What comes next, and what does it look like?
Will things ever go back to normal?
Where do we go from here?
Where's the blueprint?
What's the end goal?

We are living in one of the great defining, pivotal moments in history. God has, I believe, instigated a divine 'reboot' of the planet and human society that gives us an opportunity to step back from the brink. Change is here, accelerating and ongoing, and we need to grasp that it is a tidal wave that we either ride on or drown in.

This momentum is hastening the plan and purpose of God.

We have gone into this transition with an old paradigm but will come out the other side with a perception, culture and faith that's very different – only God remains unchanged.

Remember that between an old orientation and a new one inescapably lies a time of re-orientation.

There's a lot of 'unknown', but revelatory hallmarks of the 'new' are being given by the Holy Spirit.

This book will be perplexing and irrelevant unless you are aware that, as a planet and a people, we have 'crossed over' into a new epoch. Mindsets, priorities, processes, attitudes, and behaviour that were part of the previous era will not work effectively in the new one. Recalibration is the order of the day!

Passing through a time of transition in order to discover the 'new' is a great leveller, as all previous leaders and 'experts' are back to square one.

Neither they nor we have 'passed this way before', so we are all novices and all on a steep learning curve for which our previous knowledge and experience have not prepared us.

A wineskin is great if you have wine – otherwise it's just baggage!

Character, spiritual fruit, and intimacy with God are all we can take forward from here.

One of the things that is so helpful when navigating uncharted waters is to know what 'landmarks' to look for. This book isn't comprehensive or definitive but is a great help, as you're unlikely to have a map!

This emerging epoch will be characterised by certain traits and hallmarks, which, when you see them, will firstly bring you confidence that you are on the right trajectory and secondly help you discern between old and new wineskins.

To follow Jesus is to become more and more like Him (sanctification), and this sense of movement and journey is exemplified for us, by Him, in His life on earth.

The master key to this path is personal revelation from God through the agency of Holy Spirit. The Bible explains that the 'mature' children of God (and only those) are those who are 'moved by the impulses of His Spirit'. It is only when we experience the reality of God that we can begin to live the life that He intended us to – with all of the implications of that statement. Many of the things we are used to will fade, fizzle out, and disappear (at God's instigation), and the only way that realignment can be successfully undertaken is through a deep, personal, and authentic relationship with Father, Jesus, and Holy Spirit. It is a case of how well you know them, not how much you know about them.

Tradition and vested interest will be challenged, religion will be confronted head on (which won't be pretty!) and much will be turned on its head.

To navigate these uncharted waters without capsize or shipwreck, you will need an immovable, unshakeable, and relational anchor. The Bible is not the anchor, God is!

Pause and ponder these questions:

- **Am I ready for this paradigm shift?**

  ....

  ....

- **Am I ready for my 'non-negotiables' to be challenged, questioned, and displaced (by God)?**

  ....

  ....

- **Am I willing to abandon myself to the voice and heart of the One who is Love?**

  ....

  ....

- **Is my theology so defined and set in stone that it's immovable?**

....

....

- **Am I excited and honoured or fearful at being on earth at this pivotal moment in history?**

....

....

- **Can I discern the difference between following a religion and following Jesus?**

....

....

- **Am I dependent on Holy Spirit or on others?**

....

....

I became aware in 2011 that I was being led along a path that would involve massive change and transition, and so it has been proved. However, the magnitude and extent of that shift was way more than I expected or dreamt. Considering all that the Lord has said and shown me since then and, observing the journeys of the hundreds of others I've met on a similar road, I've come to perceive that the path of transition from an old epoch to a new one has several phases to it:

Phase 1: 'Leaving Ur'

Remember the account of God asking Abram to leave where he was and go into the unknown? Abram realised he couldn't stay put but didn't have a clue where he was going or how he would get there. He had to move forward in faith, fully trusting God.

This is the starting point that many have wrestled with, and I suspect it may be unavoidable. If you can't let go of the old, you will be unable to perceive the new. The old isn't 'bad', it's just not the new.

Phase 2: 'Detox' and wilderness

For many, this is the phase that is the most difficult. It usually involves feelings of loneliness, rejection, and the pain of being judged, ostracised, and misunderstood. There is a sense of loss, a feeling of being stripped back and being adrift on the ocean. There is inevitably a loss of some relationships which were considered close ones, and this is bewildering until you see (later) that it is part of the realignment that runs through this journey. However, the fruit of this scenario is twofold; you come to depend on God like never before, and you discover the real you.

This is also the time that God starts to help us 'unlearn' much of what we thought was settled and definitive. It is the process of detoxing the religiousness in us which would otherwise obstruct and restrict the deepening of our connection with Him.

Phase 3: 'Hello!'

After a period in the wilderness (which it seems can range from a few weeks to many years), and after the realisation that God was revealing you not testing or punishing you, a remarkable thing starts to happen. You become aware of others travelling the same road in what seems to be a random accidental connection – it's not!

It's thrilling, puzzling and created by Holy Spirit. It is the beginning of relating to others of a 'kindred' spirit rather than being joined by doctrine or label.

Phase 4: 'Repatriation'

As a consequence of the journey thus far, there comes a growing and deepening sense of where you belong. What emerges in you is a passionate, even obsessive, desire to see heaven on earth (as Jesus prayed). Your 'default' increasingly reflects the heart of the Lord as your 'go to' becomes more spiritual than earthly. More and more, time and focus are given to the values, culture, and practices of heaven until we live, securely and joyfully, in the Father's house.

We come home!

Phase 5: House dynamics

Living 'from heaven to earth', rather than vice versa, leads us to 'know' the reality of that overworked phrase 'what would Jesus do?' If you spend enough time at home in Father's house, you will eventually and intuitively come to a place of being aware in your spirit how heaven functions and what its atmosphere feels like. Being 'seated with Jesus' is offered to us as a present reality, not just a future experience.

I find that Holy Spirit is eager to be by your side as you push into these new encounters and insights – so feel free to ask Him to lead you.

Phase 6: Ambassadors

Only when the first five phases have been travelled can we then authentically represent heaven and its King in a foreign country. Meeting an ambassador allows a person to learn, discover, and enjoy much about the ambassador's homeland. The unfamiliarity of a foreign place is brought close to home by the representative from that country.

This phase reveals that it's all about heart, motivation, and the fruit of the Spirit, and has extraordinarily little to do with rules, theology, man-made church, programmes, hierarchy, or religion.

Jesus was the supreme ambassador of heaven and calls us to follow in His footsteps.

There is a cost to this road, but there is such joy and inexpressible connectivity with God that, for me, is beyond description. It will lead you to discover He who is the 'pearl of great price' in a way you never believed possible.

In recent years, I have experienced loss, rejection, isolation, slander, anxiety, fear, and betrayal; but in the healing process of each of these experiences, a door opened to draw me yet deeper into the heart of God.

In this book, I share some of the revelations that have emerged from my journey of retreat with God, and I humbly offer them to you.

The short chapters of this book are standalone rather than sequential, so it can be dipped into, with certain things that may become pertinent for you the reader. I have intentionally written in a simple, concise, and conversational way, and largely without any religious jargon or theological terms, to make the content as accessible as possible.

My longing is for you to encounter the reality of the Godhead in a more profound way than before. I want to positively 'provoke' momentum in you towards a greater spiritual maturity and a deeper and more intimate relationship with the divine (John 6: 63).

My prayer for you is quite simple – as you reach out to Father, Jesus, and Holy Spirit, in a childlike way, may you discover the richness, even ecstasy, of the vibrant, abundant life Jesus purchased for us and that we were created to live.

I pray that you discover more and more the tangible reality of intimate relationship with God and encounters that transcend information and knowledge.

From a tender heart and with much love,

Jonathan

1 Enjoying the unknown

It is improbable, if not impossible, to enter a new day unless you are willing to leave the old day behind. This is not something that most people find easy, because it requires us to leave our comfort zone and step into the 'unknown'. The emerging epoch that we find ourselves in is full of adventure into the unfamiliar, the uncomfortable, and even the scary, which is why many stay exactly where they are and maintain the status quo (whatever that means for them). Under other circumstances, this maybe wouldn't overly matter, but in this season, it will become more and more dangerous and disconnected to stay in the 'old' rather than venture into the 'new'.

Whatever the right choice is, the wrong one is to do nothing!

It is true that this is easier for some people, especially those who are wired like pioneers, but resident fear has no place in any follower of Jesus, and we have not been 'given a spirit of timidity' or fear. I'm suggesting that none of us is exempt from God's call at this time to 'cross over' into what He has prepared for us. It's reminiscent of the Israelites being asked to cross the Red Sea into the Promised Land after wandering and wondering for 40 years. I have found that if we take our own hands off, subsume our life into the one He planned for us, trust Him implicitly (that's different from theoretically), and believe what He reveals, He takes us on journeys we never ever dreamt of.

After some tentative steps, some 'risking' of possibilities, and some exercising of faith, this path becomes less and less scary and more and more exciting. A whole new world opens inside us and around us, and there comes a point where there is a lot of joy, laughter, and contentment in walking with God like this. Instead of developing coping strategies, there is a glorious 'wild ride' into new discoveries, a dependence on God, and a whole other level of fulfilment and impact. Imagine being happy to embrace the unknown, enjoy change, and discover the new without feeling overwhelmed, terrified, puzzled, or lost!

Paradoxically, it's in our utter dependence on God that we find spiritual strength and discover that our impact is often birthed from our brokenness.

We were created to revel in being continuously changed by God and forever discover more of Him. This is where our relationship with Him is deepened, where revelation is released, and where wisdom matures. I believe that this is what is in God's heart for all His children, and you too can swim in the endless ocean of His love and experience the dreams and destiny He has for you. Embrace this unknown path with Holy Spirit as your guide – you won't regret it.

The first step to getting somewhere is to decide that you're not going to stay where you are.

> 'Lord, even when your path takes me through the valley of deepest darkness, fear will never conquer me. You remain close to me and lead me through it all the way. Your authority is my strength and my peace. The comfort of your love takes away my fear. I'll never be lonely for you are near.' (Psalm 23: 4)

(Use 'My journal' at the back of this book to make notes.)

2 Heaven's perspective

As believers, we find ourselves living between two realities, the physical and the spiritual. Whichever of these realities we spend most time in, pay most attention to, and focus mainly on will shape our mindset, our thought life, our worldview, our interpretation of the Bible and our lifestyle, as well as our relationship with God. It is therefore important to perceive which has the greater influence on us, wouldn't you say?

For many, there seems to be a 'disconnect' between the biblical theory and the reality of their life, which is often caused by living in the 'wrong' reality for too much of their time.

Perspective is a choice you make!

Being a child of God and being 'seated with Jesus in heaven' means we always have the option to consider His perspective of anything or anyone we encounter. From personal experience, I can tell you that this is powerful and transformative! (It's also quite shocking sometimes.) When you view a picture or photo, there is the element of perspective – what is your eye drawn to first? Where is the focus?

We always have a choice; do we see our circumstances, situation/crisis in the foreground and God somewhere in the background, or God looming large and the rest in the background? Do you see God through the 'filter' of your circumstances, or do you interpret and perceive your situation with the revelation of who God is and what He says about you?

This really matters, as it affects the level of stress, anxiety, and fear we experience daily. Often what we consider to be 'negative' scenarios or occurrences are things that God utilises to redirect or mature us.

The 'valley' element or 'wilderness' part of our journey is transformative and is essential for the deepening of our connection with God and refining our character.

A 'God' perspective can even lead us to embrace those things that stretch, puzzle, pain, or challenge us.

There is a great illustration of this in 2 Kings 6: 11-17, which records an incident in the life of Elisha. This prophet and his sidekick found themselves in a life and death situation from which there seemed no escape, yet they chose different perspectives and so came to different conclusions. However, after God opened the spirit eyes of the sidekick, he saw what Elisha had seen – God's perspective! The facts were unchanged, but how they were viewed completely changed.

What if every time you found yourself facing a difficult or scary situation you paused before jumping to conclusions and asked God to open your spirit eyes to see things as he does? Choose the reality of heaven and bring it to earth! We are created and called to manifest the reality of God as we follow the example of Jesus.

'The eyes of your spirit allow revelation light to flood into your being.'
(Luke 11: 34)

(Use 'My journal' at the back of the book to make notes.)

3 A healthier spirit

We are a 'spirit' being with a physical body, but are we nurturing that spirit to become mature and healthy?

Since God is a Spirit and made us in His image (Genesis 1: 26) we need to understand that we are 'spirit beings' with a physical body. When we are born of the spirit (John 3: 3 & 5) and become a new creation (2 Cor. 5: 17), the Holy Spirit comes to abide within us, which is to say He comes to take up residence in our spirit (John 14: 17, 23). His presence facilitates us to develop an intimate relationship with the Lord. The indwelling Holy Spirit is the most precious gift that God has given us.

Many of us are currently navigating an ever-darkening spiritual, cultural, and political ocean filled with rip tides and treacherous currents; however, we don't need to be influenced or controlled by them. I'm so glad about that aren't you? Instead, we can swim in the living water that flows in our spirit and thus stay in the divine 'flow'. In our spirit resides the Holy Spirit, with all His wisdom, direction, vision, revelation, insight, discernment, love, peace, freedom, counsel, and joy, which are all available to us when we are in a place of intimacy with Him. From this 'secret place', we can recognise a voice or influence that does not fit in with what the Holy Spirit is revealing to us or doing in our lives. In fact, those influences do the opposite and steal our peace. They have an agenda to disturb and trouble us, to bring confusion and distress, to manipulate our thoughts and feelings and deflect us from God's heart and purposes. Satan does not care what current you are in, so long as it's not the one that flows from your innermost being (which is your spirit). I long for you to discover that staying in this flow is the secret to being entwined with God. It's integral to experiencing peace and freedom and means you are not intimidated, manipulated, or controlled by external forces. It empowers you to say 'No' to any person or force that is not aligned to what is flowing out of your spirit. In this inner flow, you are empowered to reject anything and everything that is competing for your attention, allegiance, loyalty, or resources.

You too can learn to live above fear and circumstances. It's here that you find confidence that you are attuned to what is in God's heart.

These things take time to develop, and mistakes are part of the journey to maturity. Know that these mistakes do not define you or determine your destiny but simply refine you.

> 'As you live in the flow that comes from your spirit you discover that God is able to show you that "all things do work together for good."' (Romans 8: 28)

> 'The spirit of man is the lamp of the Lord, searching all the innermost parts of his being.' (Proverbs 20: 27)

These Bible quotes, along with others many others, confirm that we have a spirit, and that is where Holy Spirit lives. Our spirit functions like a filter through which everything should pass to keep us 'in the flow' and 'on track'.

His presence inside us empowers us to be fruitful and brings us the knowledge of God's heart. It is also where we find all the spiritual resources that we need for 'life and godliness'.

Embrace Holy Spirit, and he will fill your life with an inexpressible joy, a peace beyond comprehension, an unfailing hope, and an assurance of God's love and affirmation.

> 'The mature children of God are those who are moved by the impulses of the Holy Spirit.' (Romans 8: 14)

Learning how to listen with your spirit and how to 'sense' Holy Spirit being active in your spirit are vitally important to our journey of following Jesus, and a key to our spiritual growth and fruitfulness.

Take time out to talk to and listen to God, and journal what He reveals to you.

4 Embracing mystery over certitude

Following Jesus was always meant to be holistic, healthy, holy, and humble. Religion, on the other hand, is usually a dogmatic, domineering, and dictatorial set of rules. Although both use similar language, they are a million miles apart and at opposite ends of a spectrum, experientially. These are two alternatives between which we must choose (intentionally or otherwise) and then live with the consequences of that choice.

To claim that one has a fully worked out theology, view of God, and understanding of the Bible is a sad position to be in. What that person has is an opinion (theirs or somebody else's that they adopted), a defined set of beliefs, and some immutable rules to live by. As if that wasn't sad enough, many then take on the role of 'doctrinal police' and correct or castigate anyone who does not share those beliefs and rules. Jesus encountered these people (Pharisees) and wasn't overly kind towards them.

There is such joy and freedom in discovering that this isn't following Jesus – it's religion. There is such lightness in living out of the overflow and intimacy of a relationship with Father, Jesus, and Holy Spirit. If we fully understood God, we would **be** God! There will always be mystery, loose ends, and unanswered questions, so why spend time, energy, grey cells, and emotional resources trying to work out that which is beyond us?

A young child implicitly trusts their parents without the need to know 'why' all the time. So, for us, there is less fear, anxiety, stress, worry, and heartache when we simply trust the God who loves us.

Intellectual capacity, reasoning, and logic will take us so far, but faith, spirit to spirit connection, and life will take us light years further into the heart of God, where many mysteries are revealed. A Greco-Roman mindset that places reason and the mind over spirit and experience is a primary obstacle to experiencing the reality of a relationship with Yahweh.

This seems scriptural and exciting – so why have we settled for a mental understanding rather than an ongoing encounter with God for the last few centuries? To be able to engage meaningfully in this new epoch, a shift from the prominence of the mind to the resonance of the spirit will be needed!

Learn to relax and even revel in loose ends.

If Holy Spirit brings revelation, then embrace and digest it; if he doesn't, then be still and content, 'knowing' that Father's eye is always on you and Daddy knows best. This is a simple (not complicated) transition but extremely hard for those trying to detox from the old certitude. Those who embrace this shift find an ecstatic love, joy, and peace that remain unaffected by the circumstances and situations of life.

Let go, trust Holy Spirit with your 'unlearning', and find out from Him what following Jesus is really like.

> 'Jesus said to His disciples. The mystery of the kingdom of God has been given to you who have teachable hearts.' (Mark 4: 11)

To be able to engage meaningfully in this new epoch, a shift from the prominence of the mind to the resonance of the spirit will be needed!

Take some time out to converse with God about this and journal what he shows you.

5 Leaving the status quo to find adventure

I am sure that people more qualified than I am can explain why, as a people group, Christians are, in general, so risk averse.

Is it because we have misunderstood the person and nature of God and our resulting perception of Him is one that is fear-based?

Is it because there is a surfeit of 'people-pleasing' going on that causes us to obsess about how others view us?

Is it because there is an inordinate fear of failure and subsequent punishment?

Whatever the reason/s might be, it's disabling us to participate effectively in what God is doing.

We now live in a different epoch from the one we'd become comfortable in, and familiar with. Being slow to adapt, change-resistant, or 'stuck in the mud' was an option in the past, but now it's a problem. God declares this time in history to be one of creativity, change, risk (or faith if you prefer), and new paradigms, so there is a need for preparedness to walk or leap into the unknown with alacrity and courage in response to His prompt.

Following Jesus was never once described as boring, safe, comfortable, easy, convenient, or self-serving. We have applied a process of sanitisation so that it's palatable, acceptable, and at our convenience – well not anymore!

It's important to note that this isn't about the type of person you are – outgoing and extrovert, impetuous and fearless or quiet and thoughtful, gentle and careful; this applies equally to all of us. Of course, our challenges and callings will be different, and our personality does play a part in how we engage with life and destiny. However, this is a focus on our mindsets and default settings, as it's that which needs recalibrating.

Not one of us was given a spirit of fear or timidity by our Creator – this has been acquired from elsewhere! God doesn't ask us to do something that is counter to who He made us to be, but he **is** probably asking you to be someone you may not be altogether familiar with!

It's a time to implicitly trust God, 100%, no conditions, limits, or caveats – are you willing to do that?

We find ourselves living at a pivotal point in history, and it is an incredible new initiative by God in His family and His wider creation.

Would you consider 'standing up' to be part of this momentous time? After all, He planned that you would be alive at this time to play your part.

> 'The whole of creation yearns for the unveiling of God's glorious sons and daughters.' (Romans 8: 19)

(Use 'My journal' at the back of the book to make notes.)

6 Encounter and experience more than knowledge

This is not an 'either/or' situation but a 'both/and' one!

What is shifting here is the heavy emphasis on intellect, mind, and reason at the expense of an experiential reality.

Rather than the nature and reality of our relationship with God being shaped by what we 'know', our 'knowing' becomes shaped by our deepening connection with God. Both elements are integral, but the dominance of one over the other changes everything!

Historically, we have lost the holistic engagement with God and emphasised the supremacy of the human mind. This new season is already bringing many to see the inadequacy and impotency of this situation and the realisation that 'there is more'. The revelation and realisation of this new, inverted position can only be accessed when we are shown it by Holy Spirit himself.

When the mind is dominant, it is hard to 'hear' what is being said by Holy Spirit to our spirit, and so we miss much of it. When a 'flip' occurs, and our mind is submitted to our spirit, a whole bunch of light-bulb moments happen and a completely new equilibrium kicks in.

Until it's a personal reality, it's not possible to conceive of the extraordinary difference this makes to us, both as people and as followers of Jesus. The reason why so many of us discover a new depth of relationship and connection with God in crisis is because our desperation pushes us to find solace in our spirit (where God is) because we can rarely find it in our mind. Some of us struggle with allowing 'experiences' with God to shape our beliefs (as did I for 40 years), but this is the only thing that's different from religion (Christian or otherwise). I am convinced that a great scam was embraced by the 'post Acts' church that allowed the mind to become dominant and more trustworthy and truer than the spirit, in which Holy Spirit resides.

There is a dynamism, reality, and power that lies in this whole shift that will restore 'the plan' and transform the world.

A heart that is full of love will take a person to places that a head full of theology never can.

Our God-created essence lies in our spirit, feeds our soul, and renews our mind. Discipleship is primarily a spirit journey, not an intellectual one.

> 'The mindset controlled by Holy Spirit finds life and peace.'
>
> (Romans 8: 6)

(Use 'My journal' at the back of the book to make notes.)

7 Destiny is much more than opportunity

There is a significant difference between opportunity and destiny, even if they appear similar. Of course, sometimes an opportunity is part of our destiny and something that God 'prepared for us to engage with' before time began. However, many times we are so quick to grab an opportunity that we fail to discern whether it is more than simply a way of advancement for us, our career, or ministry. This has led to the situation where there are thousands of people living as square pegs in round holes; this is frustrating and unfulfilling for both.

If you are a square peg, please check you are in a square hole to avoid spoiling your destiny and someone else's!

Therefore, it's so important to 'know' who you were created to be, to be secure in that identity, and so be free to turn down opportunities that are not part of destiny. Until you adopt this practice, it's impossible to understand the joy, freedom, and fulfilment that you experience in it.

To enjoy this way of life, there is a prerequisite to be free from the need to be needed, free of the desire to people please, and healed from the wounds of past rejection.

A great question to ask yourself is this:

Does my career/lifestyle/ministry/church/social network facilitate who I was created by God to be?

....

Another tendency of many believers is to compare themselves with others who they consider to be superior or 'more anointed'. Although there are different degrees of spiritual maturity, the putting on a pedestal of another is unhelpful at best and toxic at worst. In the long run, it blesses neither the one on the pedestal or those admiring them. Comparison is the thief of joy and the robber of destiny, so stop doing it! This practice needs eradication from the family of God. Ask Holy Spirit to show you when and where this happens in your life. Ask Him to reveal to you, in your spirit, that you were created to be a unique individual with a unique fingerprint and a unique destiny. When we 'know' who we are, we stop needing to 'perform' for the affirmation of other people.

I can't overstate what a life-transforming effect this has on those who discover it. You have permission to be fully and only the person that God created you to be.

Of course, we continue to 'become more like Jesus' from day to day, to take our negative thoughts captive, and to walk humbly with the Lord while perceiving the difference between an opportunity and our destiny changes everything!

Leaders – please help people find their destiny rather than persuading them to fill a role that suits you.

> 'We are a re-created people that will fulfil the destiny He has given each of us.' (Ephesians 2: 10)

(Use 'My journal' at the back of this book to make notes.)

8 God's rhythm

What or who determines the pace at which you live your life?

Is it work, career, family, power, status, hobbies, income, or something else that drives you? God designed us to function in a way that maximises our relationship with Him, that is of greatest 'benefit' to us, and enables us to walk in our purpose most effectively. Most people live in a hurry, too busy to notice what is happening to them and around them. There is a blessing which God promises us, that we can live from a place of His 'rest'. Busyness, overwork, distraction, and worry all militate against us enjoying this rest.

Does that sound or feel familiar?

This new season will be marked by many discovering the joy of living from a place of rest and calm. From this place comes wisdom, divine strategy, revelation, and weighty decisions. Your output will be less, but it will be of a far higher calibre and so a great deal more effective. It is vital that, as believers, we are in sync with the Lord, what He is doing, and how He is doing it. The need for a different rhythm is becoming crucial, and it needs to be aligned to His rhythm. It is time to slow down! Let God recalibrate you! This is an internal state in your spirit rather than needing to become a recluse! It's how you were designed to live; it will bring health, peace, and fulfilment to you and glory to your creator.

It's time to slow down!

'Come, and I will give you refreshing rest.' (Matthew 11: 28)

Start a journey with Holy Spirit to explore how to make this transition. Answer each of the following questions: give your own opinion on the 'Me' line, then ask Holy Spirit for His answer and enter that on the 'God' line.

- **What 'drives' me?**

  Me:..

  God:...

- **What distracts me?**

  Me:..

  God:...

- **What occupies my time?**

  Me:..

  God:...

- **What do I often worry about?**

  Me:..

  God:...

- **How much do I live in the present moment?**

  Me:..

  God:...

- **Is it lack of time or desire that's the obstacle to my finding 'rest'?**

  Me:..

  God:..

- **How can I find God's rhythm and sync with it?**

  Me:..

  God:..

Compare the pairs of answers and see where they differ. This will help create momentum for you on your journey.

9 Courage subduing fear, and coping replaced by conquering

We know that, according to the Bible, God has given us the exhortation and encouragement not to be fearful or anxious. In fact, you will find the phrase 'don't be afraid' over 365 times in its pages. Yet many believers are frozen with fear and overwhelmed by worry; why this gap between doctrine and reality? It's not that fear doesn't happen (it's a natural human reaction to some situations); it's what you allow it to do to you that is so crucial. Jesus has made it plain that no matter what our circumstances we need never be overcome by fear. So, we have a choice to make each time.

'You have not been given a spirit of fear' in Romans 8 applies equally to everyone, whatever their natural temperament is.

We have entered another period of history in which the followers of Jesus need courage. This is not some kind of stoical determination through gritted teeth to 'keep the faith', but rather a passion to be all that we were created to be and to walk in the destiny and purpose God has for us.

We have become pretty expert at creating strategies and mechanisms to help avoid or at least manage or change things outside our comfort zone. It really is time to stop doing that and maybe spend some of that time and creative energy on receiving conquering strategies from heaven. Switch from 'coping' to 'conquering'. If you are convinced that you are a fearful, easily overwhelmed person by nature – please think again! We do not need to live in fear of anything – it's the promise of God. Our part is to appropriate that truth to our lives and reject the lies of the enemy when he says otherwise. If you feel immobilised or 'stuck' on your spiritual journey, be assured that God has provided a way for you to be free from that and to know the joy of forward momentum. This epoch will be marked by the courage of many because of their passionate love affair with Jesus.

Please note that this has little to do with 'defending the truth' or correcting those who disagree with us and everything to do with living and loving like Jesus did.

What are the things that cripple you with fear or anxiety?

....

....

What does God offer you in exchange for these?

....

....

Have the courage to love the outcast and marginalised, to heal those who are sick, to care for the poor, to bring hope to the despairing, to speak peace, and to be the 'good news' to those around us.

Let's say less and bless more!

> 'Be strong and courageous. Do not be fearful, dismayed or intimidated, it's the Lord who goes with you and he will not fail you.' (Joshua 1: 9)

(Use 'My journal' at the back of the book to make notes.)

10 Sonship liberates the orphan

Let me say at the outset that this reality of 'sonship' is gender-blind today. Inheriting all that the Father has for us is equally true for both His sons and His daughters. Sonship, as defined in the culture of Bible times, described, and implied, all that went with inheriting from a father. The Bible effusively describes all the extraordinary blessings, freedom, and abundance that are ours in Jesus.

However, many Christians seem to be unaware, or have forgotten the truth, that we have access to all of God's resources and heart. Sonship is a great concept and an exciting doctrine, but it's worthless unless and until we have a divine revelation that God is our Father, and we are His sons. Teaching and expounding this truth, without it being our personal reality and experience, is both unhelpful and misleading. Theory is only useful if you practise and live out what you learn (think learning to drive).

This is the time and season for teachings like this to become authentically lived.

Less talk and more walk!

Sonship is a legal status; when you were born physically you unequivocally became a child of your parents. When we are 'born again' we become a child of God – fact. This does not mean we are a good/bad, happy/sad, or compliant/feisty child; it simply means nothing can change our legal status. This is true of our spiritual position – nothing can change that, but we still choose whether to be a child who honours our Father or not. A 'mature' son is much more than just a 'son' (status); he (or she) is living as someone who reflects their Father.

'Adoption' in the Bible is not the concept we are familiar with and is less about being accepted into God's family than it is about coming into the maturity of sonship.

Ask yourself and Holy Spirit:

How well do I reflect the heart of Father God?

....

Am I an authentic representation of my Father?

....

Do people see something of Father in me?

....

What 'sonship' blessing/benefit seems to be absent in me?

....

Is the love of Father 'real' or just theory in my life and heart?

....

Is my experience of a father/son relationship in the natural adversely affecting my spirit relationship with Father God?

....

There is so much for each of us to inherit, receive, and enjoy as 'sons' of God. The enemy, of course, works hard to rob and steal and prevent us from entering the fullness of our inheritance in Jesus.

I urge you to do whatever it takes to ensure that you regularly encounter and experience the love of Father. He longs passionately for you to 'know' Him, not simply to have an intellectual grasp of the truth.

'God released the Spirit of Sonship into our hearts.' (Galatians 4: 6)

11 Displacement of shame and low self-esteem

One of the most glorious elements of the death and resurrection of Jesus is the truth that we need never again be swamped and disabled by shame. Shame was dealt with once and for all, yet despite this, many believers are shackled by shame and guilt. Often, we acquire shame as a result of that which others have said and done to us, and it can be crippling; but it isn't how Jesus described the abundant life He intends for us.

Even if shameful things have happened to us or by us, this truth remains – you can be free from shame in Jesus. All shame and guilt can be taken to Jesus and exchanged for wholeness, forgiveness, acceptance, love, and significance. Amazing, yet real!

In this emerging epoch, we need to mature these truths into our personal reality with the powerful, supernatural help and revelation of Holy Spirit. Ask Holy Spirit to reveal to you anything that is causing you to feel shame or guilt.

....

....

....

Take those things and situations to Jesus and exchange them for the incredible alternative he offers you. Remember that what you give to Jesus you leave with Him!

When the enemy reminds you of those things again (which he will), I suggest you remind him and yourself that Jesus says they are removed as far as the east is from the west, and He recalls them no more. What gratitude rises in us for His forgiveness and freedom!

In my experience, many believers struggle and suffer with a low opinion of themselves. Low self-esteem is both painful and crippling and is a powerful tool of our enemy. Whatever the reason or cause of this perception and belief, it simply does not belong to any child of God, and it's time to allow God to eliminate that mindset. Being free of this destructive view will allow you to be fully the person you were created to be, enjoy life, and find fulfilment.

This new day will be notable for the rise of many who accept and believe what God says about them. This does not lead to pride and arrogance (unless you choose that road), but rather to stability, godly confidence, and a healthy inner life.

God's heart and plan is for you to be healthy and happy.

A Blessing

I bless you to be free from condemnation and self-hatred.
I bless you to see yourself as Father God sees you.
I bless you to see the truth that you are unique and precious.
I bless you to know that you are significant and valuable.
I bless you to know that you are the apple of God's eye.
I bless you to see that Jesus empowers you to love yourself.
I bless you to know the truth that God says you're beautiful.
I bless you to encounter and live in the reality of God's love.
Let it be so.

Holy Spirit impart the revelation of truth to my spirit. Amen.

12 Peace in storms

Most Christians are familiar with the Biblical account in Matthew 8 of Jesus asleep in a boat during a violent storm, with his disciples beside themselves with fear. Their experience as sailors and their knowledge of the lake meant that their full-scale panic was a reasonable and understandable response to the life-threatening event unfolding around them.

They forgot to factor in the presence of Jesus.

Their circumstance became so dominant that it drowned out their 'connection' to the one they followed.

We have taught for many years that Jesus offers us 'Shalom', which is beyond comprehension or rational thought, yet we frequently allow our situation to become so totally overwhelming that we find it hard to see things from Jesus' perspective. This is when our 'default' position is truly seen. This is now a time when our reality and our theology must synchronise. If you can't find peace in a storm, then you've probably forgotten to factor in God!

A spiritual truth is useless unless it's your reality as well. There are serious storms ahead of us soon, and it's imperative that we discover the secret of God's peace in our heart! These are those who will stand strong when the rest run for the hills!

It's our entwinement with Jesus, not our circumstances that must determine our response to storms.

Peace is an active and living thing that emanates from our spirit, not a mind over matter determination through gritted teeth.

Is this 'shalom' a concept/doctrine that you aspire to or your personal reality?

....

....

Let's be honest and allow Holy Spirit to show us how to live life from this place of peace.

Prayer

Holy Spirit, I ask you to take me on a path that leads me to the reality of God's peace in my heart.
I speak to my spirit and call it to attention so I'm receptive to an awakening of You in me.
I speak your nourishment to my spirit.
I receive the 'Shalom' that Jesus offers and appropriate it by faith.
Amen.

> 'The peace of God, which transcends all understanding, will guard your hearts and minds in Christ Jesus.' (Philippians 4: 7)

(Use 'My journal' at the back of this book to make notes.)

13 From performance to radiance

Performance that is motivated by the need for approval or to build reputation is a subtle but deadly trap that's been successfully deployed by Satan, not least in Christendom. Your value does not lie in what you do, or what other people think of you, but in who God created you to be.

We live in a culture (secular and church) where 'hitting targets', receiving accolades, sticking to the rules, climbing the leadership ladder, and being competitive are the norm. Achievements are not wrong in themselves, but scrutinising the motivation is essential (if a little scary). This new epoch will see these things become unimportant, even irrelevant to many, so let's be willing to let them go.

When Jesus lived on earth, it was his 'person', demeanour, power, and wisdom that caused people to be drawn to him, not his position, status, or wealth. His love was astounding, His wisdom confounded the 'wise', and he always looked at a person's motivation and heart. The only people He judged were the religious 'performers' who imposed rules on others.

What distinguishes the followers of Jesus from any other group of people is the tangible expression of Him that radiates from their person and demeanour. At this point, doctrine is something of an irrelevance; **it's how you live, not what you believe that reveals Jesus to the world around you.** Let's be so present with God that there is a radiance that goes out from us. Rather than bringing the message, let's **be** the message.

Radiance is defined as 'a glowing light being emitted from something'.

A radiant person is 'one who is so joyful in their heart that it shows on their face and makes them attractive'. The word radiant appears a few times in the Bible. Moses, after a sustained time in God's presence, was radiant. Jesus was radiant as he was transfigured in God's presence. Stephen, as he saw Jesus, had a face that was radiant as he was stoned to death.

The common thread and key here is their location in the presence of God. Everything is changed in His presence, including us!

To break free from the performance 'trap' and become a 'radiant' follower of Jesus we simply need to invest time and focus on God in His tangible presence.

> 'Those who look to him are radiant.' (Psalm 34: 5)

> 'If your spirit burns with light, fully illuminated with no darkness, you will be a shining light, reflecting the truth of God by the way you live.' (Luke 11: 36)

Maybe there is something to meditate on here that will allow God to refine and redefine how we impact our world.

We will move from our old emphasis on speaking words to a new one where it's simply our presence that does the talking.

(Use 'My journal' at the back of this book to make notes.)

14 Intimacy replaces formality

Intimacy and formality are at opposite ends of the spectrum when it comes to types of relationship. The first invades personal space, while the second stays physically disconnected and distanced.

Over many centuries of history, the church has largely chosen to relate to God much nearer the 'formal' end of the spectrum than the 'intimate' end. However, in this era, we are being called, drawn, and wooed by God to walk in greater intimacy with Him than we have done before.

This will resonate powerfully with some and be distasteful to others, depending on what they have already experienced in their walk with Father, Jesus, and Holy Spirit. To be fearful that this closeness would result in familiarity that eventually leads to a lack of respect, awe, and wonder is to completely misunderstand the 'spirit' nature of our relationship with the Three. The closer you get relationally with them, the greater the wonder and reverence that grows in your heart. In fact, you are less likely to 'stray away' when you live in this place of intimacy with God than when you rely on a detailed and thorough theology. This is not what we have previously been taught, but oh it's so liberating, so transforming, and so powerful. I would gently urge you to park some (if not most) of your doctrinal certitude for a while and see what the Lord shows you without those boundaries in place.

Don't let your intellect control what occurs in your spirit.

Adopting the posture of a novice will lead you (as it did me) into places and revelation that will stun you into silence, mature your spirit, and make you wonder why ever you previously settled for less. It will cause you to see the Bible in a way you have never done before, to realise the smallness of the human mind, and to experience the ecstasy of intimacy with Father, Jesus, and Holy Spirit. This really can't be 'taught', only experienced.

I could fill the rest of this page with further hints, tips, and suggestions, but that would be just more words at a point at which words are redundant!

There is more for you!

Be like a dog with a bone and don't let go of God and all He longs to reveal to you. He really does! Yes you!

Pursue closeness with Him like the man who found the pearl in the field and gave everything he had to obtain that one thing – the thing of great worth, the key, the prize.

> 'Continue to grow and increase in God's grace and in intimacy with our Lord and Saviour Jesus Christ.' (2 Peter 3: 18)

(Use 'My journal' at the back of this book to make notes.)

15 Custodians of creation

You might wonder why this chapter occurs at this point, but it's not an accident! An unexpected outcome of living more intricately connected to the Lord for both myself and many others I've talked to is realising the concern and heart God has for ALL that He made. God gave humanity a gift and a mandate or command to nurture all that He had made. He asks us to care for it and cause it to flourish and multiply. This responsibility has been largely overlooked by the followers of Jesus both on a practical and spiritual level. It's vital to realise that we are not 'masters' of creation – we can't rule over it at will – but custodians or stewards of a gift given to us by God.

Christians have been known to be disparaging of those 'fanatical' environmentalists who question humanity's treatment of our planet, but maybe we should put our own house in order first?

Do you accept this responsibility?

Who represents the kingdom of heaven regarding the health and welfare of God's creation?

Words need to be backed up with action!

Let's run with this commission. It is time, once again, to take up the mantle of blessing the world around us – God's creation.

Do you make declarations to counteract the harm and negativity that humanity imposes on creation and to bring 'heaven's values to earth'? It's time!

(Use 'My journal' at the back of this book to make notes.)

Declarations

I speak blessing and fruitfulness over all creation. I speak God's favour and blessing over the planet's ecosystem and atmosphere to counteract the damage and toxicity inflicted on it by humanity.

I declare that the skies, in all their splendour, reflect the genius and artistry of God.

I declare, in agreement with God, that creation is 'incredibly good', and its wonderful beauty and amazing complexity demonstrate the infinite power of its Creator. I acknowledge that you, God, are the engineer, sculptor, and artist of the earth.

I declare that the vast cosmos is a glorious manifestation of the One who created it. I declare that not only was everything made by you, Lord, but it only continues to exist because you sustain it.

I speak blessing over planets, stars, and solar systems; over rivers and oceans; over animals, birds, and fish; over plants, fruit, and vegetables. I speak blessing to the day and the night times and the seasons of nature. I speak blessing over the world's water supplies that they would be life-giving to all as God intended.

I worship you, God, for the majestic power displayed in the breath-taking wonder and splendour of your creation. I bow in awe and reverence before you.

16 Integrity

I have spent over 40 years of my life integrally connected and involved with Christian companies, ministries, and organisations. I have advised, worked for, traded with, and been on the 'inside' of dozens of these entities. Heartbreakingly, the most common thread I have encountered in these places is the absence of authentic, consistent, and godly integrity.

This is not a statement of judgement or criticism, but the factual, painful, and unavoidable conclusion of my experience.

Operating with integrity only when it is convenient or expedient to do so is hypocritical, ungodly, and unhealthy.

Integrity is defined as 'being honest, with strong moral or ethical principles which are followed at all times, even if nobody is watching'. Having integrity means you are 'true to yourself'. Interestingly, it is also 'the state of being whole and undivided'.

I believe that we are being asked to 'step up' like never before to walk in consistent, God-honouring integrity and righteousness. This is regardless of personal cost or adverse effect on our popularity and reputation. There is no place for manipulation, betrayal, partial truth, deviousness, guile, or malice – ever. Of course, many will say it's not possible to live like this consistently, which is true if we go it alone.

However, because the Spirit of God is in us, it is entirely possible to be who and what we were designed to be and that includes living an integrous life.

'The lovers of God will walk in integrity.' (Proverbs 20: 7)

'The one who walks in integrity will experience a fearless confidence in life, but the one who is devious will eventually be exposed.' (Proverbs 10: 9)

'You're only truly happy when you walk in total integrity, walking in the light of God.' (Psalm 119: 1)

'Integrity will lead to success and happiness, but treachery will destroy your dreams.' (Proverbs 11: 3)

'Righteousness is like a shield of protection, guarding those who keep their integrity.' (Proverbs 13: 6)

'Discard every form of dishonesty and lying so that you will be known as one who always speaks the truth.' (Ephesians 4: 25)

'It is God's desire that you silence the ignorance of foolish people by always doing what is right.' (1 Peter 2: 15)

'Consider the example that Jesus, the Anointed one, has given us. Let his mindset be your motivation.' (Philippians 2: 5)

(Use 'My journal' at the back of this book to make notes.)

17 Creativity

The epitome of creativity is God himself; He can't stop being creative – all the time! All humanity is created in 'the image of God', and therefore every person is creative in some way – including you! Of course, we can use our creativity for good or ill, constructively or destructively, selfishly or for the benefit of others, exploitatively or magnanimously – it's our choice. In case you are defining creativity as an art form like painting, sculpture, or music, I'd remind you that it includes many others; inventors, discoverers, pioneers, social reformers, educators, engineers, carpenters, medics, scientists, entrepreneurs, and blueprint creators to name but a few. All this creativity originates with the Creator, but its application is determined by the free will of human beings. God's creative core is evidenced in the extraordinary beauty and complexity of creation around and above us and climaxed in humanity. Inevitably, evil forces try to distort, poison, manipulate and ruin all this; again, it is the free will and choice of each person to partner with this or not.

As we enter this new era, it is important and exciting to understand that one of its characteristics is a surging, explosive burst of creativity in every way and every place. I relate to enough disparate networks to know that this has already begun (e.g., the world of commerce is being turned upside down with 'different' and creative new concepts and practices, many of which align to kingdom values). There is a tsunami approaching in the realm of music, sound, resonance, frequency, poetry, lyrics, cadence, and instrumentation.

There is a transition from 'mechanical' to 'quantum' underway.

God has 'blueprints' available for those who will accept and run with them. These will release new revelation, insight, and practice in every area of society. I have written the above to paint a bigger picture and to excite you about the time we live in. Aslan is truly on the move! Look for the manifestation of the creative that portrays and reflects the things in God's heart. There is one more thing for you, the reader, to consider and that is how you can engage fully with this shift.

a) Start by recognising the lie that says you are 'not creative'. That is to partner with evil and deny the love, care, and attention that your Creator has lavished on and invested in you.
b) Don't let others tell you what you are or are not but go and sit at the feet of Jesus and ask Him about yourself and who you were created to be (notice 'be' not 'do').
c) Be careful not to allow your preconceived ideas to deafen you to what God is showing you. Let your spirit be tender and your mind be quiet as you watch and listen.

God is doing a radical new thing and longs for you to be part of that. Trust Him – He is always good and kind.

> 'Through his creative inspiration the Living Expression made all things, nothing has existence separate from Him.' (John 1: 3)

> 'Discover creative ways to encourage others to motivate them to acts of compassion.' (Hebrews 10: 24)

(Use 'My journal' at the back of this book to make notes.)

18 Lovers not consumers

When we shop for groceries, we have a wide choice of stores, with most of us having a favourite depending on our preferences. This is also true of brands and labels. We are used to behaving as consumers because that is what we are in this scenario. We are culturally and personally familiar and comfortable with having the right to choose and the right to switch if there's something better. Sadly, many Christians have adopted the same mindset towards church. We go where we prefer the style, theology, or structure and switch if we go off it. This is so far from Biblical Ecclesia, and we are so used to it that we can't see what's in front of us. The spirit of denominationalism has flourished for centuries (spirit is not limited to denominations but exists happily in networks and streams – even progressive ones). All this is changing! There, you have now had a heads up. In this new and emerging epoch, **God is calling His people to Himself to live in a place of intimacy (entwinement) with Him**.

This has so extraordinarily little to do with dogma, doctrine, or rules and everything to do with being passionately in love with Father, Jesus, and Holy Spirit. It is rooted in encounter with them rather than in a defined belief system or theology. It is only from that close connection with the Three that we will become lovers and consequently move away from the posture of a consumer. One remarkable outcome of this is the discovery of actual unity of the Spirit and other people with 'kindred' spirits.

Think about human relationships and how relating out of love results in a different motive, attitude, and outcome than when we operate out of fear, duty, or obligation. I love to be and do what God asks because I love Him, not because I have no choice. Those two things are light years apart, even if the resulting action is the same. Let's cremate our consumer style preferences and demands, let's abandon our 'requirements', jettison our non-negotiables, and be sold-out lovers of our Beloved Father, Bridegroom, and Mentor.

Let's determine to be known as those who love with a passion and extravagance that can only have God as its source.

> 'God-lovers make the best counsellors. Their words possess wisdom and are right and trustworthy.' (Psalm 37: 30)

> 'Lovers of God have been given eyes to see with spiritual discernment and ears to hear from God.' (Proverbs 20: 12)

> 'So, live the rest of your earthly life no longer concerned with human desires but obsessed with what brings pleasure to God.' (1 Peter 4: 2)

> 'You show that you are my intimate friends when you obey all that I ask of you.' (John 15: 14)

> 'We can be sure that we've truly come to live in intimacy with God, not just by saying so, but by walking in the footsteps of Jesus.' (1 John 2: 6)

(Use 'My journal' at the back of this book to make notes.)

19 Humility

Humility is defined in the dictionary as 'being free from pride or arrogance, not having an over high regard of oneself'. This attribute is the result of a heart motivation and not to be confused with 'acting' in humility as an external behavioural action, which is false humility.

The Bible also has a lot to say about genuine humility:

> 'Be free from pride-filled opinions, for they will harm your cherished unity. Don't allow self-promotion to lurk in your heart.'
> (Philippians 2: 3)

> 'With tender humility and quiet patience, always demonstrate gentleness and generous love to each other.' (Ephesians 4: 2)

> 'God resists you when you are proud but continuously pours out grace when you are humble.' (James 4: 6)

> 'Whoever continually humbles themselves to become like a little child is the greatest one in heaven's kingdom.' (Matthew 18: 4)

The practical heart of this matter, it seems to me, is that we are intentional in ensuring we are not opinionated, haughty, or arrogant in our thoughts, words, and actions towards God and other people.

One would have to be blind and deaf not to realise that Christians, generally, have an appalling track record in this area, but that will change!

The 'new' is to be characterised by a new love, care, and heart for one another that will see godly humility restored and pride outlawed. Please resist pointing the finger at others, but consider, honestly, your own position and practice in this regard. Take some time out to ask Holy Spirit to show you where your heart is at. It is virtually impossible to display humility if it's not resident in your spirit, vocal in your mind, and active in your soul.

Transformation is from the inside out and has no short cuts.

Maybe make a note below of things God brings to your attention and then a declaration/prayer to help you 'become more like Jesus', who is our prime example of how to live in humility.

Note

....

....

....

Prayer/Declaration

....

....

....

....

....

20 Honour displaces judgement

This is something of a continuation of the previous chapter on humility. I am convinced that as part of the preparation of Jesus' bride (his followers), God is requiring us to cease from the practice of making judgements against other people and especially of other believers. This practice is widespread among Christians and will not lightly or easily be altered; but it will change because it does not have any place in the family of God. Even when truth is being spoken, it is rendered worthless if it comes out of a heart that is judgemental. Jesus always 'read' the heart, not the words. The spirit in which something is said or done is vastly more significant than the words or deeds themselves. Simply refraining from harsh or critical words is only part of what's been asked for, as this is just a vacuum. This spirit of judgement is 'displaced', not simply removed. It recedes and dissipates in the face of honour. As thoughts, words, and deeds that honour God and all that he created – especially humanity – increase, they displace the negatives. Instead of struggling and battling with not being destructive, we focus on honouring and find the negative lessening more and more. Allow the positive to grow internally, and the negative will wither both internally and externally.

You should try it! It's utterly amazing and actually works. It changes you, your relationships, your perception of and intimacy with God, and your world. You will change situations and atmospheres; people will be drawn to Jesus in you, and the kingdom of God 'will be at hand' wherever you are.

I want to say one other thing about honouring others. It is important not to confuse honour with flattery.

Speaking well of others who honour God in their lives is powerful.

Thinking the best of people is good – see the gold in them. Not allowing theological differences to become divisive is crucial. Sensing people's hearts is much more important than debating their opinions or doctrinal preferences. Loving and blessing everyone regardless of their demeanour towards you is full of grace, gentleness, and the love of Jesus.

Putting someone on a pedestal and hanging on their every word is tantamount to idolatry. 'Bigging them up', adopting their latest teaching, following trends, or flattering others to gain attention or traction must be avoided – it's corrosive. Check out everything with Holy Spirit. Honour what God is doing and those who are partnering with that.

Don't forget to honour yourself – God's precious, significant, and beloved creation. Please stop judging yourself and others.

> 'Keep your thoughts continually fixed on all that is authentic and real, honourable and admirable, beautiful, respectful, pure, merciful and kind.' (Philippians 4: 8)

> 'Be devoted to tenderly loving other believers as members of one family. Try to outdo yourselves in respect and honour of one another.' (Romans 12: 10)

(Use 'My journal' at the back of this book to make notes.)

21 Revelation supersedes information

Most times that Jesus taught on earth; he did not do so 'lecture style' but in the everyday setting using everyday language, and what He said was often somewhat cryptic.

Parables are designed to make you ponder what's been said rather than 'spoon feed' the listener.

> 'Whenever Jesus addressed crowds, he always spoke in allegories. He never spoke without using parables.' (Matthew 13: 34)
>
> 'His disciples asked Him, why do you always speak in these hard-to-understand parables? Jesus explained; you have been given the intimate experience of insight into hidden truths and mysteries of the realm of heaven's kingdom. Everyone who listens with an open heart will receive progressively more revelation.'
> (Matthew 13: 10-12)
>
> 'Jesus taught them many things by using parables to illustrate spiritual realities.' (Mark 4: 2)

This being so, how have we got to the current model of teaching and discipling that is largely about the impartation of information rather than facilitating an experience of a dynamic spiritual reality?

Even making this model more interactive doesn't really make much difference to the result.

If 'teaching' were the explanation of what you experience and encounter rather than the 'theory' of Christian living, what a different place we would be in.

This shift is a difficult transition, not least for those who 'teach'.

Whilst the academic, scholarly, theological, or studious element of learning and debate is not to be dismissed, it needs to become a small part of what is encompassed in 'teaching'.

Where are those who impart revelation from the spirit which causes a transformational shift and recalibration in the heart, mind, and life of those listening?

If you 'teach', then let it be mostly the things which are a current, dynamic reality in your own personal life and experience and not theoretical 'truth'. Let's not get stuck in an intellectual quagmire when our spirits are longing to soar.

Delving into the Bible, however deeply, is of limited use unless God is present at the time of reading/study.

Revelation from Holy Spirit to your spirit will take you to places utterly beyond any cognitive capacity.

I believe that this new epoch will be characterised by, among other things, revelation by God to our spirit that will far outstrip our intellectual capacity and dispense with our penchant for rational, logical, proven deduction. If you truly allow Holy Spirit to 'teach you', then you will find you have to unlearn much of what you already know to make room for what He will show you.

In my personal journey, the fresh insight He gives has not been what I previously thought and had even taught to others.

Whilst Holy Spirit doesn't contradict the Bible as originally written, He will inevitably challenge your interpretation of it!

(Use 'My journal' at the back of this book to make notes.)

22 Prayer redefined

Here are some observations about prayer going forward into a new day:

a) It's vital to learn to listen a lot more than you speak when you are 'with' God.

b) Much of what we ask God for, He has already offered us, but we've not accepted that invitation or appropriated it in faith.

c) Prayer is primarily a language of the spirit rather than the mind.

d) We often ask God to intervene when He has already told us that we have His authority to speak into situations ourselves.

e) Prayer is a two-way conversation/interaction, a language of love and intimacy between parties who are deeply in love with each other. It is never a function or task to be completed. (Formal prayers addressing a remote God become religious practice and an odd concept.)

f) If we sense God's heart, we can declare and speak out with confidence and faith rather than pleading with Him or even begging Him to do something.

g) Humility, silence, reverence, intimacy, worship, confidence, and dependence all sit harmoniously and happily together when our relationship with Father, Jesus, and Holy Spirit is authentic.

I guess the most important question to ask **yourself** at this point is, 'Do I know how to communicate from my spirit with Holy Spirit?'

This extraordinary journey must begin with that spirit connection between us as a 'spirit being' and God who is Spirit.

One of the outcomes of this new, relational expression of prayer is a fresh revelation of what is called 'intercession'. Many are gifted and called by God to intercede (stand in the place of), and they are diligent and persistent in their crying out on behalf of others. However, the challenge of the new era requires us to let Him recalibrate our thinking and past practice. It's less about begging God and repenting (although both have a place and significance) and more about declaring with faith, and in our God-given authority, heaven's values and culture here on earth. I believe that if the love, heart, time, and energy of all intercessors switched from pleading to declaring, the transformation in the world would be seismic. Obviously, there will be times when it is right to contend, to 'travail', and to wrestle, but I am convinced these are to be the exception rather than the rule! Please take some time to listen to God on this matter.

Prayer/Declaration

The longing in God's heart is for me to 'know' Him with an intimate, personal connection and oneness.
Father, I want to encounter your fathering.
Jesus, I want to experience the overwhelming sense of your embrace, as a Bridegroom embraces the bride.
Holy Spirit, I long to sense your permanent presence in me and beside me.
Amen

(Use 'My journal' at the back of this book to make notes.)

23 Persecution

The honour of suffering!?!

This is just one of those things we don't really want to think about; anyway, is it relevant in the western world in the 21st century?

Have you considered the possibility that you may witness, sooner rather than later, believers suffering exclusion, abuse, torture, and even martyrdom in your lifetime in the UK and Europe?

If you know that you are chosen by God to live in 'such a time as this', then you know that being grounded in Him and walking by faith, in courage, is an essential lifestyle. Godly wisdom and discernment in this matter will be much needed in order to be prepared and without fear.

How do you feel about the possibility of being treated unfairly or even persecuted for being a follower of Jesus?

I'm amazed that it's a surprise to many to discover that Jesus says we should count it an honour and a privilege if our own journey includes suffering as the consequence of our allegiance to Him.

How do you feel about that?

Ask Holy Spirit how you can prepare for this possibility/inevitability?

The biggest issue in this scenario is how to be positioned spiritually, so as not to be overwhelmed by fear. Fear is a natural, protective instinct and emotion so in itself is not wrong. The Bible tells us 365 times not to be afraid, so the expectation is that we will have plenty of opportunity to choose whether we succumb to fear or not.

Persecution, in whatever form, is something we, as followers of Jesus, will experience to a degree we have not previously known.

If this scares you to the point where your fear takes over and you stick your head in the sand, it is important that you start a dialogue and journey with Jesus asap. Mature believers need this to be a 'settled issue', not least so we can empower and counsel younger generations to be prepared.

In 2018, I persisted in my questioning of the Lord about a viable model for Ecclesia in the future. His reply took me aback; 'The only "model" which is viable beyond the short term is the model of the underground church'.

> 'All those who choose to live God-honouring lives, as worshippers of Jesus, will experience persecution.' (2 Timothy 3: 12)

> 'As God's children, we prove ourselves authentic in every way. For example, we have great endurance in hardships and persecution. We don't lose courage in a time of stress or calamity.'
> (2 Corinthians 6: 4)

> 'And because you follow me (Jesus), you will be on trial before kings and governmental leaders as an opportunity to testify to them in My name.' (Luke 21: 12/13)

> 'Don't lose your bold, courageous faith, for you are destined for a great reward!' (Hebrews 10: 35)

> 'Remember what I have told you, a servant isn't superior to their master. Since they persecuted Me, they will also persecute you.'
> (John 15: 20)

(Use 'My journal' at the back of this book to make notes.)

24 Generosity

There will be an emergence of a generous and extravagantly loving spirit that will dislodge the 'poverty' mindset that has plagued many Christians for so long. This is not based on the level of wealth a person has but on simply being obedient to the nudges and promptings of Holy Spirit.

I must admit that for my wife and I this has been a challenging learning journey over the last decade. We loved being generous from a place of having resources but found it hard to be on the receiving end of generosity when life took an unexpected turn. Being willing to accept people's unexpected and generous support was uncomfortable for us, but that was only the start. Very slowly we have learned to give and bless, regardless of our resources or bank balance, and every single time over the last decade God has 'covered' the actions that we took in response to Him. It's true that having wisdom accompany this way of living is advisable, but God is never anyone's debtor. We had to 'push through' the insidious voices that talked about being irresponsible, reckless, presumptuous, and naïve to reach a new normal. This renders tithing a redundant activity, as everything is His (as opposed to 10%) to be deployed as He directs.

An interesting observation we have made is that doing what Father asks has resulted in us giving to people rather than organisations. It seems that, based on our experience, **investing in God's kingdom is not the same as investing in a church!**

I encourage you to maybe 'unlearn', with the guidance of Holy Spirit, your 'view' of generosity in general and the gifting of money in particular.

Generosity is not limited to money but applies to other resources too. Investing time in others to encourage and empower them to be fully who they were created to be is a privilege and an honour.

Most Christian leaders regularly find themselves being drained (as a pastor) or even bled dry by some of the people they attempt to help (I have been there on many occasions).

This rarely happens if you **invest only in the people Father asks you to!** When he was on earth, Jesus loved everyone but invested in relatively few. He partnered with what he saw His Father was doing and set the example for us to follow. If at first this feels a little callous, elitist, or discriminatory, it's because you're transitioning to a different paradigm. We are still called to be kind, loving, respectful, and forgiving to all of humanity – that's different from walking beside and investing in those who God planned to be part of your destiny.

> 'Let giving flow from your heart, not from a sense of religious duty. Let it spring from the joy of giving.' (2 Corinthians 9: 7)

> 'A stingy Sower will reap a meagre harvest, but the one who sows from a generous spirit will reap an abundant reward.'
> (2 Corinthians 9: 6)

> 'God is more than ready to overwhelm you with every form of grace so that you will have more than enough of everything.'
> (2 Corinthians 9: 8)

> 'Our love can't be an abstract theory we only talk about, but a way of life demonstrated by our loving deeds.' (1 John 3: 18)

(Use 'My journal' at the back of this book to make notes.)

25 Contentment not comparison

Experiencing the abundant blessing of life itself as a gift from God is precious and transformative. This is soured and distorted when we engage in the practice of comparing ourselves with others, their circumstances, popularity, influence, gifts, or ministries.

Many think that lack of resources or platform are the issue, but the real problem is comparison. When we try to fill our emptiness with 'stuff' or achievement, we are merely papering over the cracks.

We must lose the compulsion to measure ourselves and our lives by looking at others. When we just revel in the experience of being alive, we begin to discover the eternal reality of abundance, joy, fulfilment, and love. This changes our perception of pretty much everything but especially of ourselves. Remember, we are co-heirs with Jesus over all creation, with no need to slavishly run after the hollow, shallow, and temporal trifles that so many chase after.

You were not designed to feel empty, insignificant, or fearful – the Creator has said so!

So, where is the disconnect and why?

Why is there a chasm between our reality and the one offered to us by God?

You are alive, so you can touch, smell, see, and hear what is around you. It's important to heighten these senses and live with an appreciation of the present moment. It is utterly amazing to sense the vibe of creation as it honours its creator. As in the natural, so with the spiritual; you have been given ears and eyes to discern and sense what is happening around you. Ignoring them is perilous, as it leads to 'missing' what God is revealing. Being intentional in 'cultivating' both natural and spiritual senses will make an enormous difference and save you a whole heap of trouble.

Can you perceive that your life here on earth is but a segment of an eternal continuum?

All that we need to live our life to the full has been provided by the one who gave us that life and whose breath is at the very core of our being. Our collaboration with God, if it's unconditional and intentional, will bring us to a place of exuberance and joy regardless of the circumstances of our life.

Being content whether in a 'place of plenty' or a place of need is to know one of the mysteries of heaven. It creates a remarkable stability and groundedness that alters the way we do life and sets us up for eternity.

To summarise, let's abstain from comparison and relax in contentment.

> 'Don't be obsessed with material stuff but live content with what you have, for you always have God's presence. He promised you, I will never leave you alone.' (Hebrews 13: 5)

> 'I know what it means to lack, and I know what it means to experience abundance. I know the secret of overcoming all things – in fullness or hunger. It's in the strength of Christ's explosive power that infuses me to conquer every difficulty.' (Philippians 4: 12)

> 'A tender, tranquil heart will make you healthy, but jealousy can make you sick.' (Proverbs 14: 30)

> 'I am humbled and quieted in Your presence. Like a contented child who rests on its mother's lap.' (Psalm 131: 2)

(Use 'My journal' at the back of this book to make notes.)

26 Fruit matters more than gifting; maturity redefined

Just to be clear, the fruit I am referring to is the fruit of the Spirit as listed in Galatians 5: 22/23. Specifically, **Joy** that overflows, **peace** that subdues, **patience** that endures, **kindness** in action, a life full of **goodness**, **faith** that is full and prevails, **gentleness** of heart, and **strength of spirit.** What an incredible list of active expressions of being entwined with God and demonstrating His attributes.

In recent decades, there has been a strong emphasis in parts of the church on developing and exercising spiritual gifts, although with varying amounts of success and with considerable collateral damage.

In this new paradigm, however, the call is to be more focussed on growing 'fruit' in our lives. If many of those with 'gifting' had more fruit in their lives, their gifts would be a lot more effective! For example, a prophetic word that comes from a kind and wise heart is of much greater value than when it does not. Many people whom God has given giftings struggle because they do not have the character (fruit) to support it.

It is not gifts that are the hallmark of maturity (however great they are) but fruit.

Pause and consider that statement and any ramifications for you.

It's time to replace questions like:

> 'What is your gift?'
> 'Is your ministry developing?'
> 'How many followers do you have?'
> 'How are you serving this church?'

with others where we encourage each other to be more 'fruitful'. Questions such as:

'Am I or are you kinder, more patient, gentler, more self-controlled, fuller of faith and mercy than last year or last month?' This is how we measurably gauge our ongoing maturity as a child of God.

This is not an 'either/or' situation but a 'both/and' one. However, the emphasis and pursuit are significantly different from before.

The fruit that characterises your life and ministry are more important than your ministry gift itself.

This is the whole purpose and goal of sanctification – to become (however slowly) more and more like Jesus, in a measurable, noticeable, tangible way. It's not the external exercise of a gift but the heart and motive in the spirit of the one ministering.

Pause and consider this and how it might change your perception and practice.

> 'The mature children of God are those who are moved by the impulses of the Holy Spirit.' (Romans 8: 14)

> 'When your life bears abundant fruit, you demonstrate that you are mature disciples who glorify my Father.' (John 15: 8)

> 'Those who are mature in their faith can be easily recognized, for they don't live to please themselves but patiently embrace others in their immaturity.' (Romans 15: 1)

*Speaking in tongues is a gift of the Spirit.
Controlling your tongue is a fruit of the Spirit!*

27 Fragility and resilience

There persists in Christendom the erroneous idea that weakness and vulnerability are negative traits (especially for leaders) and that we must 'grow beyond' them. This has led to the manipulation, exploitation, and even abuse of many thousands of people by those in positions of power and influence.

***N.B.** Dominance and leadership are NOT synonymous but are diametrically opposed to each other!*

A mother and father will be vulnerable when a 'manager leader' will not.

It's simple but challenging to implement our calling to 'follow Jesus' and his example.

Was he strong or weak? Was he resilient or not?

....

Was he dependent on Father or strong enough himself?

....

Was he aloof and remote or did he make himself vulnerable?

....

When was he not meekness incarnate?

....

Why did he not feel the need to defend himself when falsely accused or judged?

....

Have you discovered what it's like to follow the example of Jesus? What is the difference between 'fragility' and 'weakness'?

....

....

What is the difference between vulnerability and fragility?

....

....

What is the difference between strength and meekness?

....

....

Are you someone who dominates or is dominated by others? Neither of these scenarios is a healthy place to live.

Ask Holy Spirit for true revelation of how you are positioned.

To be secure in our relationship with God, to know Father's affirmation, Jesus' love and power, and the constant friendship of Holy Spirit means that there is no fear in vulnerability, no need to people please, and no need to establish our place in any 'pecking order'.

It's so clear in the teaching of Jesus that we can live in a way that seems bewildering to others. We find resilience in dependence on God, confidence from a humble heart, strength birthed in weakness, vision from intimacy, and revelation in stillness.

In this new day, we must learn a new way (which is really the original way) to be vulnerable without being fragile and to be resilient but because of our complete dependence on God.

> 'My grace is always enough for you and My power finds its full expression through your weakness.' (2 Corinthians 12: 9)

> 'I am the vine, and you are my branches. As you live in union with me as your source, fruitfulness will stream from within you – but when you live separated from me you are powerless.'
> (John 15: 5)

> 'He humbled himself and became vulnerable. He was a perfect example.' (Philippians 2: 8)

28 Knowledge and Wisdom

Knowledge is the acquiring of information. It's about knowing many things and getting the facts sorted out and bedded in. This is fine as long as you are aware that all the data in the world does not of itself equate to wisdom. Wisdom is generally puzzling to the intellectually proud yet appears to be more accessible to the 'poor in spirit'. Wisdom sees many things differently, rather than knowing many things factually. It seems that truly wise people know how to be present, which is the 'one thing' needed for wisdom to flourish. Today, we possess more information than at any previous time in history, yet at the same time we have less wisdom. We need to recover the skill of keeping our heart open, our mind quiet, and our mouth shut. This explains why the same Biblical extract can bring a loving person to a deeper love but an egocentric person to an interpretation that facilitates control and feeds division. This is so evident when we consider the Pharisees; although they were God's representatives, were religiously observant, and 'knew' God's law perfectly, they always missed the reality of a present Jesus. This was despite the fact that He was stood in plain sight before them. Sadly, there are many who still do this today.

> 'Spiritual blindness is not uncommon, and many are "seeing but not perceiving" and "hearing but not understanding."' (Acts 28: 24-27)

> 'You search the scriptures because you think you will find the truth, but the truth is a person who stands before you.' (John 5: 39)

Knowing in our spirit means something entirely different from knowledge in our intellect.

When something we have known in our head is experienced or encountered in our spirit, it moves from being *the* truth to being *our* truth. It transforms from being something we believe to something we unshakably 'know'. The Bible states that God is love because of what He has done and who He is, but when you encounter/experience His love as a reality not just a concept, it changes everything.

Many fail to distinguish between the two and settle for the first when God longs for us to experience the second. Head knowledge is valuable after you encounter God but can be misleading before it.

Whether your 'knowing' is intellectual or in your spirit, there is a precious gift that leads to maturity and that is wisdom. Having knowledge and/or revelation is amazing, but it becomes powerful when coupled with wisdom. Many a true word has been spoken with a lack of wisdom that has minimised its impact, effectiveness, and benefit for the hearer/reader. The great news is that God specifically tells us that if we lack wisdom we can ask and receive it from Him.

> 'Wisdom is a gift from a generous God, and every word He speaks is full of revelation and becomes a fountain of understanding.'
>
> (Proverbs 2: 6)

> 'The wisdom that is from above is always pure, considerate and teachable. It never displays prejudice or hypocrisy in any form.'
>
> (James 3: 17)

(Use 'My journal' at the back of this book to make notes.)

29 From prophetic words to fulfilment

Many of us have, in recent decades, been privileged to hear or even bring significant prophetic words; scripture also contains many prophetic words as yet unfulfilled. Obviously, by definition, these words relate to the future until their day of fulfilment is reached, but how do we know when that is?

If we become so familiar with prophecies always being in the future, we may well not notice a shift as they become applicable now.

As with all else, the answer lies in our listening to Holy Spirit, who will tell us when a 'now' time has arrived. Once we have this 'heads up', we are able to declare a word with faith and expectation in a way we couldn't before.

A recent example of this was the Lord highlighting for us a verse in Malachi 4:6 where it prophesies that 'the hearts of the parents will be turned to their children, and the hearts of the children to their parents'. Holy Spirit explained that 'now' was a time when that word would be fulfilled if we stepped into it. We started declaring (with real expectation and faith) that the fulfilment of this promise would now be made manifest in the lives of those we know who are struggling with family estrangement (we named each one and spoke over them either in person or as if we were together). Dozens of situations resolved quickly, often after years of hard and painful relational breakdown – it was both enthralling and humbling!

We must engage with the prophetic with expectation and wisdom, otherwise it is of little use or blessing to either giver or receiver. Complacency, frustration, and disappointment need to be intentionally rebuffed, as they will mitigate against faith and hope.

Timing is God's business more than ours, and rarely do the two time frames match! It is vital to be sensitive to Holy Spirit prompts and timing in regard to the prophetic and its fulfilment. It's not a case of twisting God's arm to bring a word to fruition when we need or want it, but about being ready to partner with Him when he tells us it's 'now'.

It really is worth starting a conversation/dialogue with God about this to see if He wants to 'change your perspective', release strategy to you, or ask you to partner with Him in specific declarations. Why not start now?

> 'Abraham waited patiently in faith and succeeded in seeing the promise fulfilled.' (Hebrews 5: 15)

> 'As we wait, we trust in God's royal proclamation to be fulfilled.'
> (2 Peter 3: 13)

> 'Fear and intimidation are traps that hold you back. Place your confidence in the Lord , you will be seated in the high place.'
> (Proverbs 29: 25)

(Use 'My journal' at the back of this book to make notes.)

30 An eternal perspective

We live in two realities whilst on earth, one physical and one spiritual. The big question is which of these is the dominant one that affects and determines our thoughts, words, and actions?

Seeing events, situations, relationships, dreams, opportunities, and even crises from the perspective of eternity will radically alter our perception of them and their significance. This eternal perspective can only be perçeived in our spirit rather than our mind, will, or emotions. This is not complicated to grasp but seems 'out of reach' until it's encountered and then practised.

Living in both realities (as we must) isn't in question, but asking which one is shaped by the other is a huge question for you to consider. To see one's life in the context of eternity will lead to decisions, conclusions, and actions that many will not understand or even appreciate.

Many of us, for many years, have been shaped by our worldview, our theology, and our culture, which, in practice, has meant our physical reality dictating to our spiritual one. Generally speaking, local church has been shaped far more by the 'earthly' reality than the 'heavenly' one, which is why it has reached the parlous and perilous condition it is currently in.

A 'church' or an individual believer promoting the concept of following Jesus but doing so without the power of Holy Spirit will be unable to adapt to be part of the next, vastly different 'move of God'.

To filter everything in this life through an eternal context will facilitate the coming of 'heaven on earth' just like Jesus prayed.

It will be less about effort and drive and more about flow and internal serenity. This then births peace, abundance of joy, and contentment, rather than stress, burnout, and angst! Which would you prefer?

All of this may seem great, but you're thinking how this can be done practically. Like many other things described in this book, it comes down to being in a place of entwined intimacy with the Three. If we allow God to loom larger than what life throws at us, we will find it easier to see 'what He sees'. If it really feels beyond your reach (which in reality it isn't), then may I suggest you find others with the same desire, on the same journey, and engage in 'mutual' encouragement, accountability, and support. Alternatively, ask God to show you who can 'mentor' you for this part of your journey. Significant numbers of these 'mentor' Mums and Dads have already been released by God to do exactly this.

(You can email the author at jbugden@hotmail.co.uk if you have difficulty finding someone)

> 'We view our slight, short-lived troubles in the light of eternity. We see our difficulties as the substance that produces for us an eternal weighty glory far beyond all comparison.' (2 Corinthians 4: 17)

> 'Keep a constant watch over your soul, pray for the courage and grace to prevail over the things that occur in life.' (Luke 21: 36)

(Use 'My journal' at the back of this book to make notes.)

31 A motivation to contribute rather than acquire

This hallmark will be found most obviously in the 'marketplace' where 'business' is conducted. In this time of great shift when we collaborate with God to restore and establish 'heaven on earth', the question of how to do business is under scrutiny and review.

How do we 'trade' in a way that reflects and honours the One we follow? Once again, the underlying foundational question here is 'what is the motivation?' The heart, culture, and 'order' of heaven is steeped in love, with God, who is love, at its centre. It promotes, perpetuates, and practices unconditional, unending love and kindness, the 'preferring' of others, and a burning desire to honour, bless, and empower those God created. This description painfully brings into sharp focus just how much we are at odds with the kingdom of heaven here on earth.

This is a really good point at which to pause and ask yourself – when I conduct business, whether on a tiny or huge scale, how do I do that and what motivates me when I'm engaged in it?

Make a note of your thoughts and anything Holy Spirit shows you

....

....

....

This may have a ring of utopian ideal to you, as it did to me, but that's largely because we start from a place of distorted teaching and thinking. Imagine the impact and culture that would be generated if God's people conducted themselves and their business in a way that was radically counter-intuitive and counter-cultural. I believe it would cause a real stir!

Trading is an opportunity to express collaboration, unity, and 'loving our neighbour' as well as bless and empower others to be who they were created to be.

Wanting to do business because it will benefit, prosper, or enhance the activity and success of another party is rare to find, yet it is the expression of the heart of God.

What is your most common motive – giving or acquiring?

'What can I bring to the table replaces what do I get from this.' This is not a complicated transition, but it is very counter-cultural and difficult to adjust to. Accompanying this massive shift will be the emergence of 'changed hearts' that will drive forward 'a different way'. Genuine integrity, humility, and generosity will emerge as hallmarks of a way of being and acting that powerfully reflects the values of the kingdom and its King. There will be a move from formal, institutional, managerial, hierarchical leadership models to more informal, consensual, and peer-oriented ones. Wanting to see others succeed becomes a high-value goal and reflects the heart of a father.

People before profit becomes the priority (God's favour follows our obedience, so profit is a consequence more than a goal).

Competition is redefined as we outdo each other in our 'contributions' rather than our acquisitions. As believers, it's of far greater eternal significance that we make an impact than an income (of course there is nothing wrong with wealth until it becomes the primary goal and driver).

> 'Be devoted to tenderly loving your brothers and sister. Try to outdo each other in respect and honour.' (Romans 12: 10)

> 'Let "giving" flow from your heart, not out of a sense of duty but from the joy of giving to another.' (2 Corinthians 9: 7)

> 'It is much better to have little, combined with much of God than to have fabulous wealth and nothing else.' (Psalm 37: 6)

32 Outrageous love and the ministry of reconciliation

One of the consequences of living a life of constant companionship with Father, Jesus, and Holy Spirit is the tenderising of the heart. Kindness, compassion, and empathy 'rub off' on us when we stay close to the Three. We don't have to engineer it or work hard to develop it – it is the natural (supernatural) by-product and outworking of our intimacy. This dissipates striving and trying to do better and births a flow of peace and fulfilment as we partner with God in what He is doing and saying.

It is stating the obvious to say that the love of God is outrageous, as it is both unconditional, and unending, is not based on our performance or behaviour, and is indestructible. The challenge for the followers of Jesus is to replicate this way of loving His creation – most especially other people. In the time we have now entered, I believe we are being called to radically change how we think about and interact with our fellow human beings. This is a specific invitation from Father as well as a biblical principle to love God with every part of our being and then to love others in the same way. I remind you that you can't love others if you dislike yourself!

It is this outrageous, extravagant love that will galvanise a great spiritual harvest and prepare believers for the return of Jesus.

I believe that God is requiring this of us, not merely suggesting it would be nice!

Are you in?

....

It is natural to feel that this is beyond us, so we question the point in engaging with it.

Jesus told us that we will do 'greater things' than he did because the Holy Spirit lives inside us. The same power which raised Jesus from the dead is alive inside each of us, and it enables us to make godly choices.

If you have spent much of your life in the local church environment, you may well find the previous sentence difficult to agree with – what about my weaknesses, sin, and failures you may ask. My intent is not to change your theology but to cause you to pause and ask Holy Spirit whether He wants to renew your thinking.

You **can** walk in signs and wonders, and you **can** impact your world! You **can** love like Jesus!

The poor choice that many Christians have made in recent decades is to 'chase' and desire power rather than the one who is the Giver of that power. This love is dynamic, revolutionary, anti-religious, and the essence of God. Its presence and activation in our lives is the result of entwinement between us and Them.

This love displaces judgement, criticism, and pride, and it flushes out our religious tendencies, as they are all incompatible with it.

This love is also what empowers us to fulfil the ministry that God gave to all His followers – the ministry of reconciliation.

Only from this 'position' of agape love can we hope to bring the reconciling heart of God to our world.

'God has made all things new, reconciled us to himself, and given us the ministry of reconciliation.' (1 Corinthians 5: 18)

'The love of God will be perfected within the one who obeys Him. Then we know we've truly come to live in intimacy with God.'
(1 John 2: 5)

(Use 'My journal' at the back of this book to make notes.)

Author's note

In the next few chapters, you will find considerable overlap as I approach the same core topic from multiple angles.

The transition we are caught up in is so pervasive and comprehensive yet so counter-cultural to our previous perception and reference grid that it's difficult to perceive and get our head around. It is a shift in thinking that can only be countenanced from a place of revelation to our spirit.

Whilst these chapters have application to individuals, they also have pertinence as we explore what the new 'wineskin' might be like.

We don't dishonour or discredit the old wineskin, but please don't expect to find new wine there!

It is hard enough to shift a mindset, but changing a long-established culture is something else, and we need to allow God to be the architect of this.

There is such abundance, joy, freedom, and peace that lies ahead on this path.

33 The surrender of control to focus on empowerment

Whilst self-control is evidence of Holy Spirit sanctifying us, any control of another person is ungodly (except in a few exceptional situations).

The local church has been riddled, hampered, and crippled by the wrong control of persons by others for centuries, but that is being replaced by a vastly different style of leadership.

Nobody 'owns' another person.

The heart of a father or mother for their children is to see them flourish, prosper, and reach their full potential, to be happy and fulfilled. There is a contentment that eliminates competition and comparison and seeks the highest good for those we love.

Instead of exploiting or pressuring (in the nicest possible way of course) someone to help you fulfil your mission or calling, let your heart of love spur you on to ask yourself how you can become more fully the person God created. Let's help others to find their true purpose and destiny and give them the freedom to explore and develop that, regardless of whether that will benefit ourselves or not. If this became common practice among believers, a whole new dynamic expression of local church/community would emerge.

So called 'accountability' and submission to leaders has been grossly abused in Christendom, and it's led to a weak, impoverished, and disillusioned body of people, as well as to insecure and manipulative leaders. Both of these groups have perpetuated this sad state of affairs rather than allowing Jesus to be reinstated as head of His Church. This is a moment in time when this situation is no longer tolerable or fit for God's purposes and will change at His instigation. There is little purpose to be served by blaming others or criticising leaders, so ask yourself the question rather than pointing the finger at others.

Be brave and ask Holy Spirit to show you how you've been complicit in this distortion of truth and misrepresentation of Jesus.

....

....

> 'God has empowered us to conduct ourselves in a holy manner and with no hidden ulterior motives. God's great grace enables us to minister to others with pure heart, not in the clever wisdom of this world.' (2 Corinthians 1: 12)

I can say, from personal experience, that seeking to 'release' people instead of trying to persuade, convince, argue with, or control has been an unmitigated joy and privilege. To be motivated by a desire to see others reach their full potential in God, to discover their purpose and destiny, and to be free of 'baggage' is a million times more enjoyable and effective than the alternative.

The conviction that the only way to maintain order and propriety within Ecclesia is to place rules, regulations, and requirements upon others is misplaced (to say the least!). Every human has the same value, is created in the image of God, and has a voice to be heard. Leadership that implies the superiority of one over another is ungodly and must find no place in 'church'. Of course, there are challenges when we allow all to play their part, but that is no excuse for domination or manipulation.

(Use 'My journal' at the back of this book to make notes.)

34 Institution to fluid community

The God-ordained order that exists in heaven is the result of rhythms and patterns that flow from the union, honour, and relationship within the Trinity. Structures, systems, and programmes are man's poor attempt to reflect this 'order'. If we are to bring 'heaven to earth', then this divine 'order' is meant to be part of that.

Earth has a society that is deeply divided and has an 'elite' with a desire to 'subdue' any who disagree with or obstruct them. Most structures and systems are built to facilitate control, to empower the few, and are characterised by greed, selfishness, arrogance, and pride. There are myriad 'institutions' in the world that foster, protect, and perpetuate these ungodly goals.

This is the starkest of contrasts with heaven's 'order', which exudes unity, harmony, peace, and is rooted in unconditional love.

I believe that God is in the process of allowing these institutions to crumble and decay, to falter and stumble, and to lose power and influence. This is because they do not serve the kingdom of God at this point in history (even if they once did).

It is hard to overstate the enormity of this change that God has initiated. When Jesus completed his mission on earth, nothing was ever the same again. He changed everything and completely fulfilled/replaced all the previous rules, practices, and culture. The seismic magnitude of change that is occurring now is not unlike the one that happened 2,000 years earlier!

Thankfully, God has promised to reveal His alternative to each of these corrupt entities, which will grow as the 'old' falls. He asks us to be watchful, to wait, and to listen as He initiates this seismic transition.

There is a wonderful, gentle, honouring atmosphere that emerges once this managerial control is done away with. There is fluidity, spontaneity, and unpredictability embedded in this 'divine order' that is exquisite and glorious, yet it freaks many people out. As I've said repeatedly in previous chapters, this joyous possibility requires that we be in intimate union with the Three.

Gladly surrendering to God is not the same as submitting out of duty, fear, or obligation.

Grudgingly allowing others an equal value is vastly different from 'preferring each other in love'.

Allowing God to be in control of our lives and our gatherings means that we do not have control!

Does your thinking need Holy Spirit updates?

....

....

....

Note to leaders

It is time to let go of control masquerading as leadership.

Dominance and leadership are not synonymous!

Structure rarely serves God's purposes unless it has the capacity to shape-shift and brings freedom to people rather than restriction.

Leaders, please release others, don't demand their loyalty, and move beyond your need to be 'followed'.

> 'Don't be controlling and dictatorial but influence others by your example as you lead with compassion, tenderness and from a heart under God's leadership.' (From 1 Peter 5: 2 & 3)

(Use 'My journal' at the back of this book to make notes.)

35 Family not hierarchy

Our model, as Christians, in regard to 'family' without hierarchy is found in the Trinity, whether that is 'nuclear' or 'church' family. Father, Jesus, and Holy Spirit are distinct, united, and honour each other; they express different aspects of the Godhead – all this but without hierarchy. There is no seeking prominence or domination among them, no 'jostling for position', no concern over status, no arguing over role. They are content to be themselves and let the other two be themselves too. They are so 'together' that they appear as ONE.

In the context of local church leadership, there is a vast difference between:

1) those whose authority is derived from the title they hold, the job they do, the position they have, the power they exercise, or their strength of personality.

2) those whose authority is simply an expression of who God created them to be.

It is so important to know the difference!

The Biblical concept of 'five-fold' ministries can only be effective when it is perceived as sequential rather than hierarchical.

It is nigh on impossible to introduce 'family' into an existing structure that operates as a hierarchy. This is a massive issue for those responsible for local church, as the majority of those entities are hierarchical in nature and practice. It is a case of walking away from an old model in order to engage with a new one. It's the organisation that is the problem – we don't walk away from others in the family.

Whilst the UK is a European nation by virtue of it being in the continent of Europe, it is no longer part of a corrupt, unfit, ungodly organisation! We don't leave THE CHURCH, but we CAN disconnect from a church structure that is no longer fit for purpose. The wonderful thing about family is that no matter the mess or the problem blood relationships are strong and can overcome the odds. I love being in the family of God and getting to know and love so many of my brothers and sisters, but I don't need a church entity to do that – in fact, it's harder in that context because of all the structural and political baggage. When family functions as it was designed to do, there is a security, a love, an honour, and a freedom for each person to be the person they were created to be. Even when there are disagreements, the motivation of loving others in the family will prevail.

Loving each other is more important than agreeing with each other!

The dynamics of my own family are a helpful model for me in this regard. Our three children are now all adults with their own families, so I have no control over their thoughts, actions, or decisions. They are free to live their own lives without interference or manipulation from me, even though when they were young I asked them to follow my lead and instruction. I now have no rights over them! I love them and they love me, and that takes precedence over everything else. They will often ask for my advice or wisdom, but that is entirely their choice, and they will tell you that based on their experience of me my input on certain things is worth asking for!

Wow wouldn't church communities look different if they lived like that!

The new 'wineskin' will see parenting replace management.

If you are a 'leader', please stop 'managing' people and start loving them like your grown-up kids.

(Use 'My journal' at the back of this book to make notes.)

36 Governance in the new era

Above all else, kingdom governance is now to be irrefutably relational in character, motive, and practice. There are those in the kingdom who God created to exercise authority; it's important not to throw the baby out with the bathwater! The answer to poor, controlling, harsh, ungodly governance is not to abandon all leadership but to reflect the heart of God and live and love as ambassadors of heaven.

This is quite different from what has been and has a different set of hallmarks. Here are some of these:

- It is grounded and soaked in love.
- It's more about heart motive than ability.
- It will empower not control.
- It's organic rather than organisational.
- It will feel fluid rather than rigid.
- It will be adventurous rather than risk averse.
- It won't be about following the trends of Christendom but waiting with heightened anticipation of what you, yourself, will be shown by God.
- It will be much more spontaneous than prescriptive and institutional.
- It has a sense of reality and is dynamic not dogmatic.
- It is facilitated by network not a hierarchy.

- Followship is voluntary rather than imposed.
- It's mysterious more than mechanical.
- There is a greater focus on reality than on theory or concept.
- There will be leaders who are honest not secretive, transparent not manipulative, and humble not dominant; they will be meek, wise, and gentle, loving not religious, mature not insecure, vulnerable but not fragile. They will have a priority of revelation over reputation.
- Personal lives that are centred around the presence of God, seeking, and running with God's plan, not personal agendas.
- Leading will become about equipping rather than nursing others, about growing disciples, not building a church, and about loving people rather than recruiting them.
- There will be less emphasis on the intellectual and more on the spiritual.
- Enabling encounter not just imparting information.
- An emphasis on spiritual fruit more than giftings.
- The ruthless elimination of egocentric, self-serving, unaccountable, high-profile, hypocritical leadership.
- Leadership becomes about Fathering and Mothering rather than managing.
- It will be gender, age, race, and creed 'blind'.
- Leaders will be 'recognised' by those they live among rather than simply elected or appointed.
- Godly authority is innate rather than trained for or learned.

This is not a case of only having leadership that is perfect – obviously! But Jesus, as head of His church, is inviting those who He created to have spiritual influence within it, to exercise that influence in the same way that He does – with overarching and overwhelming love, kindness, and wisdom.

> 'Jesus said, "The greatest honour and authority is reserved for those who have a humble heart. The leaders who are elevated are the most important ones in your eyes, but in the kingdom, it is the humble who lead. Am I not here with you as one who serves?"'
>
> (Luke 22: 27)

(Use 'My journal' at the back of this book to make notes.)

37 Purpose before programme

As churches have become more organised and efficient in recent decades, they have developed more and more sophisticated programmes on pretty much every aspect of Christian life and practice. Some of these courses have been very successful in helping people to grow in their understanding of Christian beliefs, in grasping theology, and in learning how to 'live by the rules'. All of this has its place and use; however, our relentless focus on 'learning' has diminished our engagement with what is even more important than information, which is encounter with and experience of the reality of relationship with God. We have largely persuaded ourselves that knowing 'about' is pretty much the same as knowing relationally – it is not! It's time to encourage people to encounter and then take the understanding and revelation God has given us to explain and firm up who and what we have encountered.

Teach to explain experience, rather than teach in the hope that one day it may be experienced.

One of the outcomes of this emphasis on knowledge has been to create a church organisation that is way too busy and way too full of programmes and activities. It's led to a priority of keeping the church organisation and diary active and attractive. This pulls people into filling roles to perpetuate the vision and output of that particular church and its leadership. That in itself is not wrong, but it has an outworking (usually) that is incompatible with God's heart and kingdom. That consequence is to assume that believers are to be put to work, serve, and commit time in the church. The question should not be 'What can you as an individual believer do for this church?' But rather 'How can we help and support you to find and fulfil your God-given purpose and destiny?'

This is such a shift that it's easy to misunderstand or dismiss – which is what I believe will happen as God turns things on their head. Far too many Christians are serving another person's vision rather than pursuing their own innate, created core calling.

I do understand if you think this is a bit hard to swallow, but I do urge you to ask Holy Spirit about this whole thing and let Him speak into your open mind and heart.

....

....

God invites us to be full of perseverance and faith, not to a man-made entity but to Him and His kingdom.

Who does God say you are? How are you fulfilling that? I want to see you reach your God-given potential, and I ask you to let me do the same. The dynamic interaction that results will both surprise and delight you.

It will lead to an expression of Ecclesia that you never dreamt would ever happen.

> 'God says, I know the plans and thoughts that I have for you, plans for peace and well-being and not for calamity, to give you a hope and a future.' (Jeremiah 29: 11)

(Use 'My journal' at the back of this book to make notes.)

38 Gardeners instead of Builders

When I first heard God say this phrase, in relation to how things will change, I admit I scratched my head a little. Over several weeks, it began to be unpacked and became an amazing analogy to help us reposition, renew thinking, and consider 'a better way'. Most of us know that Jesus said 'I will build my Church' yet spend our lives working hard to 'build' it for him and are then shocked and disillusioned when we burn out in 'His Service'.

Revelation reveals that a rethink is required.

It is so important to distinguish between a church organisation and the church of Jesus Christ. Building and expanding organisations is not necessarily building God's kingdom. There is some overlap but not a lot!

The mindset, perspective, and modus operandi of a builder and a gardener are quite different.

A builder handles inanimate materials, whereas a gardener handles mostly living, organic plants etc.

A builder relies on the skill to construct, whereas a gardener has to rely on the climate, weather, and conditions as well as their skill. A builder has detailed plans, precise measurements, and exact requirements with little 'wiggle room', but a gardener has a much greater level of freedom to be creative, spontaneous, and adaptable. A building is set, once constructed, but a garden is always developing, changing, displaying in different ways in different seasons.

Rather than interfering with what the Master Builder has said he will build, let's 'tend', nurture, and tenderly care for those that the Master Gardener has planted in our area of the 'garden'. Discover the joy and excitement (if you haven't already) of flowing in partnership with the Head Gardener. It is radically different from doing our own thing (godly though it might be) and asking God to bless and prosper it.

Be sure you know the difference!

The Bible is full of imagery around seeds, plants, fruit, and trees; it's amazing how much revelation and wisdom can be gleaned.

I reiterate that I'm not criticising what has gone before, just highlighting that it is largely no longer fit for purpose in the light of this God-initiated new era.

There are people that God has planted within your area of His garden (sphere of influence) that He destined you to bring to their full, mature potential and display His glory. He designed us to do this lovingly and tenderly, just as a gardener respectfully and gently handles plants.

Given that God has invited you to take up this calling and purpose, I urge you to re-evaluate where you invest your heart and time. It's good not to assume that you know already what God has destined you to be doing at this time; in the past, our assumptions have caused us to miss the chance to partner with Him. This is a new time – it's time to revel in what God is asking you to partner with Him in.

Please don't say 'it's too late for me', as that is simply not true – it's a new day to discover and enjoy!

Pause and ask Holy Spirit if you are currently operating as a 'builder' or a 'gardener'.

39 Big is no longer best

It's not that 'big' or 'mega' in itself is bad, but it will become vital to perceive that our obsession with being the biggest (church, mission, organisation, or ministry) that we can be will take us down a dead-end road. This wasn't the case in the season we are transitioning out of, but it is true of the emerging one.

Small is best!

There are many who have heard and felt God's heart as he calls us to be prepared for what lies ahead. Both as a society and as churches, we have been dedicated to the idea that 'the bigger the better' is the goal. We contended that 'this will increase our influence and enable us to shape society for the better and we'll have more clout and a louder voice'. This may previously have had some validity – although with only scant success – but it is now out of kilter with what is emerging.

Small, stealthy, adaptable, fluid, able to change quickly, highly relational, home-based community is replacing the highly structured, organised, fixed, institutional, slow to adapt or change, risk-averse church we are used to. Spirit led not programme led; family not organisation.

If, as I've already mentioned in this book, God has shown you too that 'persecution' of His people is imminent, then much of this makes real sense. Big, highly visible church or ministry will become virtually impossible to maintain, will become more and more marginalised, or worst of all swallowed into 'state-approved' religion.

It is so important to hear from the Lord yourself (not just via a speaker or a book) about all this. The apparently random way in which God is connecting people 'spirit to spirit' is the new 'alternative' (or wineskin if you prefer) that He is creating, and He is doing so with minimal reference to organised church. This connectivity is birthing and fostering powerful, honouring, and lasting relationships between people. It is something I encounter every day, so whether you are aware of it or not, it's already happening, and it's thrilling, stress-free, and fun!

God is inviting us – with some urgency – to make our homes places of worship, sanctuary, love, and revelation. Influence in God's kingdom is not connected to size or strength, but to obedience, dependence, humility, and intimacy. Small is so flexible and quick to respond or to change shape and alter logistics; it spends little time in debate and analysis but looks for and facilitates momentum, joy, and fulfilment for everyone.

Time to swap the oil tanker for a yacht!

This is not a novel idea but an important element in the blueprint for the era we now occupy, and I urge you to listen to Holy Spirit without condition, presupposition, or a fixed theology. I promise you that if you do this He will surprise, shock, and challenge what you thought you knew!

> 'I'm committed to walk in the way of integrity and honour, especially in my own home.' (Psalm 101: 2)

(Use 'My journal' at the back of this book to make notes.)

40 Encounters not lectures

It is rather stating the obvious that head knowledge is of limited value or impact unless the truths we have learned have become reality in our personal experience. However, many of us have, for centuries, mistaken intellectual knowledge for spiritual experience, information for revelation, theology for wisdom, and belief for relationship with the divine.

To hear many sermons, teachings, or debates, to read dozens of commentators and theologians will all increase the information you hold about being a member of the Christian faith. If this is not paralleled and corroborated by personal encounter with God, which makes it a reality, it is of extremely limited value. Many Christians have been hoodwinked into thinking they know God when what they actually know is things about Him.

Knowing about God and knowing God are two vastly different things.

Ask yourself the question, 'which "knowing" do I have more of?'

....

Then ask Holy Spirit the same question.

....

If it's not real for you, then it's just a belief or concept.

Having said all this, it's easier to see why we, as individuals and as Ecclesia, need to allow God to shift us from placing primary importance on knowledge to experience. It's time to stop teaching theory to people and start facilitating encounter with God for them. Then teach to explain and enhance what they have experienced. It may sound like semantics, but I believe it's utterly different and produces vastly different fruit and outcomes.

As believers, we must take personal responsibility for our spiritual health and growth and not blame others for our lack of either. Encounters face to face with God and a heart of love will take you way beyond anything you can comprehend with your mind. Spiritual experiences will reveal things that cognitive capability never will. So, it's good to feed our minds but not at the expense of reality; it's good to have our mind renewed but from our spirit, not from increased information. It's time to stop pretending and get real – however painful that may be. If Holy Spirit is your guide, mentor, friend, and revealed, you will be entirely safe. Ask Holy Spirit what obstacles are hindering you living in the fantastic, glorious reality of constant entwinement with the Three.

Pastor/Teachers – please don't teach theoretical revelation but only what is already a reality in your own life. Let your personal encounters with God ignite and shape how you equip and encourage others. Let's not deal in secondhand or borrowed revelation. Knowledge doesn't bring transformative life in itself – an encounter between our spirit and God's Spirit does that.

I hope I have gently 'provoked' you, whether leader or not, to start conversing with God for greater revelation and wisdom.

41 Ambassadors replace Recruiters

This new era will be so different from what has gone before, even feeling like it's the opposite. Many of us now have a deep longing to partner with God in bringing His kingdom from 'heaven to earth' and are realising that it's less about what that entails logistically and more about our motivation. God looks on the heart, but we have placed emphasis on our activities (often called ministry). For hundreds of years, Christians have focussed on getting people to church to get them saved and to grow the church. That's the motivation of a recruiter – success is measured in numbers and bums on seats.

What is now emerging, as recruitment becomes irrelevant, are those who have spent enough time being 'seated with Jesus in heaven' that their very existence on earth brings an echo of heaven. The heart is the heart of an ambassador representing the homeland. They are focussed on extolling the virtues and treasures of 'home'. Their priority is to represent their homeland well, to honour the place and the people they love, and to do it with passion and authenticity. When you engage with an ambassador, you encounter something of the land, culture, wisdom, and creativity of the place and nation they call home. Imagine if, as followers of Jesus, we were to be so preoccupied with demonstrating (not just talking about) the joy and life of our homeland and its king that we forgot to criticise everyone else and major on the things we disapprove of.

Can you picture that? What an utterly different perspective.

In this new era, two hallmarks of what we used to call 'mission' or 'evangelism' will rise. Firstly, people will equate us with what we are 'for' rather than what we are against, as at present. Secondly, displaying the love of God will become our obsession rather than correcting what and who we consider to be in error. A recruiter wants to 'win souls', whereas an ambassador wants to represent his extraordinary and loving King and His kingdom. We owe people an encounter with God (someone once said). Once again, it's a great time to stop and ask Holy Spirit about your heart and motivation.

....

....

....

....

....

Discover the thrill of representing 'home' well and bringing something of heaven to earth.

Know the joy of people encountering God because they encountered you.

It's your heart not your words or teaching that manifest the reality of God and His love of people.

> 'We are ambassadors of the Anointed One who carry the heart and message of Jesus to the world.' (2 Corinthians 5: 20)

42 Religion is the enemy!

This statement may seem obvious, but it is widely misconstrued. There is an element of the religious in all of us that we are blind to until Holy Spirit reveals it to us. The language and rationale of religion sounds familiar, plausible, and acceptable because the counterfeit looks and feels a lot like the real thing! When Jesus was on earth, most of his opposition came directly, or indirectly, from the people who 'represented God' – the religious leaders. Yet in their spiritual blindness, they failed to see the fulfilment of all they taught when He was stood in front of them. The very people who were regarded as 'experts' in serving God, and teaching others, were peddling something that was devoid of life.

The greatest obstruction and resistance to what God is doing in the 21st century will come from within what we have called 'church' and will be sponsored and inflamed by a spirit of religion.

This is a repeat of what happened when Jesus came to earth.

Having the 'form' without the reality of relationship creates an illusion that many believe is the genuine article when sadly it's fake. It is time to partner with God and allow Him to ruthlessly root out, remove, and banish anything that is the manifestation of the religious spirit, firstly in us as individuals and then in our collective expression. If we sit at the feet of Jesus (not just someone who says they represent Jesus) with patience, open mind, tender heart, and an alert spirit, it is astonishing and humbling to hear what he says – and it's often what we least expect. The Holy Spirit is present, willing, and able to be the perfect, gentle, and personal guide, teacher, and imparter of revelation. Why would anyone decline this invitation to flow with the divine?

Most readers would agree that religion isn't what God is wanting; the issue is what is real and what is not. Don't assume you aren't religious.

I challenge you to ask Holy Spirit to highlight to you any element in your thinking, speaking, or doing that emanates from a spirit or mindset of religion rather than from an intimate awareness and entwinement with the Three. This requires us to be 'teachable' (by Holy Spirit), to have a quietened mind and a sensitive spirit, and to park (at least temporarily) our dogma, doctrinal convictions, and our 'pet' interpretations of scripture. Will you try doing that?

Find a time and a place to see what happens.

....

....

....

> 'You were included in the death of Jesus and have died with him to the religious system and powers in this world.'
>
> (Colossians 2: 20)

> 'Beloved children, our love can't be an abstract theory we only talk about, but a way of life demonstrated through our loving deeds.'
>
> (1 John 3: 18)

> 'Beware the hypocrisy of the Pharisees. It permeates everything they teach and do like leaven.' (Luke 12: 1)

> 'These people honour me only with their words, but their hearts are very distant from me.' (Matthew 15: 8)

43 Oneness that is real

At a time when God is again revealing how passionate He is about His children being 'as one', it's apposite to re-evaluate and redefine what spiritual 'unity' actually means. One key passage from the Bible to grasp in your **spirit** is John chapter 17.

We are not told to create unity as it's not our responsibility; we are asked not to break it when God creates it.

This unity is not created by doctrinal uniformity, intellectual agreement, a common enemy, or belonging to the same organisation, but rather it is created by Holy Spirit and, at least initially, is an entirely 'spirit' connectivity. My spirit relationship with God and your closeness to Him mean that a 'oneness' occurs between us without either of us contributing to it.

Unity comes from alignment, not membership, and will never be 'lowest common denominator' in calibre.

Previous structures have been constructed around common creeds rather than alignment to what God is currently doing and saying. Creating new versions of these cul-de-sacs so you can 'do it right this time' is exhausting, disappointing, and futile in this new era. Alignment leads to complementary and high-impact assignments as an expression of unity in the body.

Incredibly, I have heard repeatedly over the years:

"God told me to start a 'new' church group so we can be more united." This, as a concept and strategy, is at best ironic yet has been widely practised for centuries. Even when undertaken with the best of motives, it eventually does little other than reinvent the wheel. It's pointless to pursue unity by increased division, unless you believe that unity is something that is purely organisational.

Once we shift from thinking we have a responsibility to 'create' oneness to realising it already exists and our passion must be not to 'break' it, the horizon and practical outworking of 'Ecclesia' is dramatically different.

This is an internal change in the individual before it can manifest within a collective or community context.

Initially, this different 'connectivity' can be construed as elitist or exclusive: it's not – that is an understandable misinterpretation. The Bible refers to us as being like living stones in a building of many stones – but any individual stone is only 'touching' or connected to a handful of those stones. All stones are of equal value and part of the building, but we are 'united' with just a few. Jesus loved everyone and had many followers but only did 'life' with a handful.

Our historic understanding of unity is flawed – it is time to allow God to reveal its true nature to us.

> 'Father, I pray they will be joined together as one, even as you and I are one. I pray for them to become one with us. The glory you have given me I have given them so that they will be joined together as one and experience the same oneness that we enjoy.'
>
> (John 17: 21 & 22)

44 Deconstruction

You may or may not be aware that there is, in some circles, a great deal of use and misuse of the word 'deconstruction'. Therefore, I need to clarify what I mean when I use it. I heard a prophetic word that caught the attention of my spirit during the first pandemic lockdown: God saying, **'those of you who have been asking for revival, I have answered your prayers, it's here and it's called deconstruction.'** Assuming you have read much of this book already, this is unlikely to be shocking, but it pulled me up short at the time. As we are now living in a God-initiated 'reset', everything is undergoing change both internally and externally.

I believe from my own journey in recent years that a significant and ongoing hallmark of this new era is having to 'unlearn', 'unthink', and 'unpractice' much of what has gone before.

We have a new paradigm, perspective, and 'normal' in our lives that will affect every element of our being and life, not least spiritually, if we allow God to implement it. Although it may seem daunting at first, if you undertake this metamorphosis with Holy Spirit, you will be safe and loved in your dependence and intimacy.

It is not possible to take parts of the old wineskin to re-utilise in the new one!

God stays the same, but everything else (including us) will be changed, transformed, sanctified, restored, released, and freed!

It's a different day.
It's a new era.
It's a seismic shift.

It's a revolution.
It's a new orientation.
It's a new frame of reference.
It's a change of season.
It's a Kairos moment.

It doesn't matter what phrase you choose as your preference, but to be an ostrich and bury our head in the sand will benefit nobody and won't glorify and magnify the magnificent Three!

Don't just believe what I am saying; instead, ask God and see what He says. I do ask you one thing – please don't do nothing; revelation, wisdom, and vision await those who ask, seek, and knock.

Between an 'old' orientation and a new one lies the path of 'disorientation'. Embrace it.
Ride the thermals; don't attach an engine.
Be wind-powered, not mechanically propelled.
Step off the map and run free.
Yield quickly to God but not to anyone else.
Outlive and out love the rules.
Know the voice of the Shepherd.
Tend the garden; don't build an edifice.
Leave the 'box'.
Let your sanctified imagination run wild.
Be who you were created to be!

Ask Holy Spirit to personalise and oversee your deconstruction.

....

....

....

....

45 A love revolution

It's probably true to say that most Christians know that of all the people groups on earth it is they who are to heed the call of Jesus to love God, others, and all that He created. As Jesus was the epitome of love in what he thought, said, and did, so we are called to follow in His footsteps. He even said that it would be our love for each other that would demonstrate/reveal Him to the world at large. This is widely known and accepted across the church spectrum.

Love trumps everything!

I hardly need to highlight that the family of God has missed the mark by a million miles when it comes to being loving, both as individuals and most certainly as a religion. It is, however, not for me to point the finger at anyone but to examine with honesty my own heart and motives. I simply ask you to do the same.

God's love is unconditional, so mine must be too.
God's love is never ending, so mine must be too.
God's love does not discriminate, so nor should mine.
God's love is covenantal not doctrinal, so mine needs to be.
God's love is kind not harsh, so my love should mimic that.
God's love is uniting not divisive, so mine must be too.
God's love is selfless, so mine should be too.
God's love is pervasive, so mine can be too.
God's love has no agenda or hidden motive, so nor should mine.
God's love is outrageous and extravagant, so mine can be too.

God is more than loving; He is the essence and personification of Love itself. He can do nothing else than love. Even His justice is saturated in, and motivated and birthed by, Love.

Friends, this is NOT an unobtainable, unachievable way to live but the example of Jesus we are to follow and implement in the power of God, who is living in our spirit. Everything we think, say, and do needs to be marinated in and motivated by the love of God. Let our motivation for everything be love. God is asking us to partner with Him to see a love revolution impact the universe.

It is time!

The greatest hallmark of this new era is love – first, second, and third. It will overarch and overreach and overcome absolutely everything else.

> 'Love is large and incredibly patient. It is gentle and consistently kind. It refuses to be jealous, does not boast about achievements or become self-inflated. It abstains from shame and disrespect and is not selfish. Love is a place of safety. Love celebrates honesty, it seeks the best for others and never gives up. There is faith, hope, and love but love surpasses them all.' (1 Corinthians 13)

> 'Our love for others is our grateful response to the love god has shown to us.' (1 John 4: 19)

> 'Live in obedience to God. To walk in love toward each other is the unifying commandment we've heard from the beginning.' (2 John 1: 6)

(Use 'My journal' at the back of this book to make notes.)

Words to the 'wise'

Permission is granted . . .

Following the death of her cub, a mother bear remained by its side for three days without moving. The combination of grief, disbelief that this could happen, and her instinctive loyalty made her blind to anything else. Eventually, the bear realised that she faced a stark and painful choice to either die beside her cub or leave it behind and seek life again. To remain at her post would have been of no value to what had died, and it would have prevented her from finding her future destiny and the fulfilment of being a mother again. Once the death had occurred, her loyalty, whilst totally understandable, was now misplaced and very detrimental to her. It is right to mourn, but there comes a time to move on to find new life.

What is it that you are sitting beside that you are unable to move on from?

What misplaced 'loyalty' has created inertia in your life? What future are you sacrificing by remaining by the 'corpse' of what has died? On the other side of the pain lies the fulfilment, abundance, and destiny God planned for you from before the world began. Don't be robbed of that. Your fragility is an opportunity for God to display his strength. Give him your grief, anger, disappointment, disillusionment, and fear and receive in exchange, peace, contentment, healing, comfort, hope, vision, and courage. Let what God has placed in your spirit override, feed, heal, and soften what is troubling your mind and creating turmoil in your emotions. Please don't be 'seeing' but not 'perceiving', or 'listening' but not 'understanding'.

Move on!

Permission is granted.

See and hear clearly

Position yourself so you are ready to declare that:

I AM is not a belief system.
Following Jesus isn't a religion.
Love is a state of being not a doctrine.
Verses from the Bible are not the truth – Jesus is.
Unconditional love has no conditions whatsoever.
Grace excludes nothing.
This life isn't a rehearsal for the next one.
Knowledge without encounter will deceive.
Mystery is integral, not a puzzle to be solved.
Salvation isn't about a ticket to heaven.
Questioning is healthy, not naughty.
These things will divide; to some it will be freeing and life-giving, and to others it will 'stink'.
Stand ready, positioned, and without wax in your ears!

Recalibration is required

The path through deconstruction to abundance, freedom, and intimacy with God is not easy.

As we grow into spiritual maturity, it slowly dawns on us that the parameters we choose to live within shape our belief and practice and are limiters of both our identity and our destiny. When we are given revelation as to the real expanse of God, we quickly realise that our 'box' is ridiculously small.

Many make the decision to accept that box, with all its flaws and restrictions, whilst some choose to pursue a wider, deeper, and costlier road. Moving beyond the system doesn't mean we are walking away from Jesus; in fact, it often signifies the opposite.

To perceive heaven's ways, culture, worldview, atmosphere, and intentions, we must push beyond our historical, institutionally endorsed creeds, doctrines, and dogmas.

Of course, we must guard our heart and not take it upon ourselves to judge the path of another.

However, we must take responsibility for our own path in response to the one who calls us to walk it. He never wants us to follow out of obligation but from a heart that knows His love, His grace, and His empowering. If we find the road uncomfortable, costly, or difficult, or, worse still, we can't see the way ahead, if His voice appears to take us 'off-road', we have a choice to make. Do we choose the tried and trusted path or follow Him and carve out another way?

Sometimes we stay on the old (and, for us, wrong) path because we've been taught that it's our obligation to do so, but is it?

It is the unprescribed tracks that the religious vehemently oppose and ridicule, and that's not pleasant if we are called to travel that route. If our journey is not on floodlight tarmac and well signed, if it carries uncertainty and a lack of planning, guess what, it means we really do have to 'walk by faith' in complete dependence on our Guide. There is such freedom and joy walking the personal road that He calls us to walk, even if we are misjudged and misunderstood by others.

For those brave ones who are following our heavenly Guide who knows where, I urge and plead with you to keep going; He will never leave or abandon us, and we will find who and what we are created to be!

You are so on track and part of an explosion of courageous explorers, pioneers, and 'way' makers. Your life is meant to be exciting, abundant, and influential, simply by being the 'you' God intended.

Many feel the necessity for a 'statement of faith' to articulate their faith, but often it's a poor substitute, and our concept can be compromised by words 'about' God which we believe in and then call faith. The life of faith is only and always in communion with Him. It begins and ends not in a formula of words or a set of beliefs but in Him. When we rely on a statement about God, we are not led to encounter. Instead, we end up in a place of doctrinal semantics and profitless debates, arguments, labels, and division. This is not what is in God's heart for his people. It is now time to jettison our propensity to nitpick over words and our need for verbal correctness, otherwise we will not move beyond words and discover the reality that they point to. Walking in faith is done from our spirit with our spiritual senses, fully alert and with a mind that is renewed from our spirit.

It is not what we know but who we know that matters!

Don't be confused – see clearly

Don't muddle:

Knowledge and wisdom.
Concept and reality.
Soul and spirit.
Revelation and information.
Heart and head.
Meekness and weakness.
Remorse and repentance.
Rest and inertia.
Maturity and status.
Surrender and submission.
Honour and flattery.
Vulnerability and fragility.
The Church and a church.
Selfishness and self-care.
Fathering/Mothering and managing.
Love and duty.
Behavioural change and transformation.
Destiny and opportunity.
Familiarity and intimacy.
Significance and reputation.
Relationship and religious adherence.
Recalibration and trend-chasing.
The Living Word and the written word.
Innate gifting and training.
Discipleship and religion.
Organic and organisational.

Bask in intimacy with God

The love and goodness of God is not simply a concept or just a Biblical truth but is available to be our daily reality, our experience, and our delight. Everything changes when this revelation becomes 'heart knowledge' as opposed to simply head knowledge. Being overshadowed by the goodness and presence of God for real leaves us ruined (in a good way!) for anything less. To encounter intimacy with Jesus is to be left breathless!

Read the following passage from the Bible out loud, and let the enormity of the love of God saturate you mind and heart.

> You are so intimately aware of me Lord and you read my heart like an open book. You perceive every movement of my spirit and see every thought before it even enters my mind.
>
> You formed my innermost being, shaping my delicate inside and my intricate outside. You wove them all together in my mother's womb. I thank you God for creating me so mysteriously complex – it's breath-taking!
>
> How thoroughly you know me Lord! You formed every part of me in the secret place, carefully and skilfully shaping me from nothing to something. You saw who you created me to be before I became me. By your power in me I can walk through devastation, and you revive me. You are in my past, my present and my future whether I'm aware of it or not.
>
> O God your thoughts of love towards me are more than the grains of sand on every beach. It amazes me to meditate on these things!
>
> (Extracted from Psalm 138/139)

You were created to uniquely display the essence of your creator, and your arrival on earth was timed to the second by Father God – you are not an accident, not an orphan, not insignificant, or forgotten. Let God show you how precious, significant, valuable, and chosen you are!

Change of specification

God is creating a flotilla that will circumnavigate the planet bringing in the knowledge of His glory.

He has released a new blueprint from heaven of a vessel differently designed that is ideal for the new day.

It has:

- A new kind of power for propulsion.
- A different cargo.
- Different dimensions.
- Different navigational instruments.
- New routes that were previously hidden.
- A payload, but it is not passenger-carrying.
- Adaptability.
- 'Under the radar' stealth.
- An attractive appearance.
- A new form of communication.
- Creation-friendly components.
- No user manual, as it's intuitive.
- A 'shoal-like' synchronicity.
- Resilience.
- Longevity.

Fear Fighters

Do you get overwhelmed by fear? My love expels all fear.
Are you puzzled?
My wisdom creates contentment with not always knowing.
Feeling frustrated?
It's about being not doing.
Are you miserable or disappointed?
Practice gratitude.
Do you struggle with feeling a failure?
Come and let me enlighten you as to how I see you.
Feeling trapped?
I ask for loyalty to me but to nothing else.
Are you isolated?
I set the lonely in families, which I do in my timing.
Do you feel insecure?
In the heart of Father is complete security.
Feeling rejected?
I know what that feels like. I am enough; you don't need to people please.
Have you lost a reputation?
My affirmation of you is total.
Do you feel washed up?
My new era brings you new purpose.

Do you worry that you've 'missed it'?
You haven't!
Are you tired?
Find my rest.
Wanting things to go back to 'normal'?
The best is yet to come.
Be brave.
I am leading you on an unfamiliar path, but it's Me!
Are you scared for the future?
Then live with me in the present.

Get used to different

Handy hints going forward into the unknown new:

- Intimacy feels self-indulgent till you find it.
- Rest feels lazy till you discover it.
- Outrageous love feels risky till you try it.
- Humility and meekness seem subservient till they become the default.
- Authenticity seems scary till it's familiar.
- Mystery feels unsafe till you are full of wonderment.
- Doubt feels wrong till it leads to deeper revelation.
- Kindred spirit rather than 'like-minded' seems weird before you find out how exciting it is.
- Trusting Holy Spirit seems dangerous until you discover the joy of hearing Him loud and clear.
- Being guided by spirit more than intellect appears unreliable until it's a reality.
- Not having a map seems weird until you fly free.
- The kingdom is incredibly counter-cultural to the old norm and mindset.
- Whatever the 'new' looks like it does not look anything like the 'old'.

Entwined with the Three

These are the gentle questions from the Three

Can you sense our excitement?
Can you hear our heart?
Can you perceive our intent?
Can you see what we see?
Will you love like we love?
Will you show the honour we do?
Will you stop for the 'one' like we do?
Will you partner with us in the restoration of all things?
Will your deep, entwined fusion with Us carry you through trial and persecution?
If you surrender yourself to our care and design you can fly!

From the Three

It is in lowliness that you'll find contentment. Contentiousness is not something that is imputed to you from Us.

Meekness is strength under the control of love; it's not weakness but wisdom to be meek.

Self-control, kindness, patience, and emotional intelligence are vital. If you don't have that, just come sit with Us and we will explain how.

There's no room for cynicism now, just the wide-eyed wonder of a child.

A pandemic of love will be released on earth – will you be part of it, no matter the personal cost?

Jesus is calling the Father's family home.
Father is calling the Bride to be ready for Jesus.
Holy Spirit is beside himself with excitement.

Divergence

There is an increased divergence occurring between those who see the 'Emperor' as naked and those who admire his 'new clothes'.

These different perspectives are not the same but opposite.

Divergence is not division; it's the revealing of what already is. It's the costly road to purity.

Only divine wisdom, insight, and revelation enable people to perceive the truth.

What's now called correct, necessary, appropriate, and immovable by the religious is rarely part of the kingdom.

A borrowed or adopted revelation is hollow and impotent.

A proud, arrogant, rational stance is at odds with God's longing for you to be childlike.

What many called authentic at this time is counterfeit.

Much is not what it appears to be.

I invite you to see what I see.

Come close, catch every whisper from Holy Spirit, and watch hope and anticipation rise inside you.

This is the time to answer the call to see and hear in your spirit.

Perception

Do you see but not perceive?
Do you hear but not grasp?
See and hear from a different vantage point:
Darkness is the ideal environment for light.
Illumination can only take place when there's ignorance.
Revelation can only occur when there is blindness.
Healing only happens when there are wounds and sickness.
Honour can only happen when there is difference and diversity.
Inspiration and hope intrude upon apathy and hopelessness.
Vision is often found against a backdrop of despair.
All is not as it seems, my child, so be wise and listen to Me.

My journal

My journal

My journal

My journal

My journal

Other titles published by **spirit level communications**

OUCH!

Heresy, masquerading as theological truth, has been a successful strategy deployed against the church for years. The clever twisting of truth has resulted in many being duped by the counterfeit; they have then settled for so much less than God intended and Jesus purchased.

Following Jesus? – A reality check

We live in a different world and a new kingdom paradigm; especially in comparison to the one many of us had become familiar with. The recalibration needed to get into the 'new flow' is immense and challenging – even bewildering to some. As followers of Jesus we must see that this is a time to be on a 'love' offensive, not a time for being defensive. It's a time to re-evaluate what our 'non-negotiables' are and whether they align with God's heart.

BOOM!

What we say, whether to ourselves or others, to situations or even hopes and dreams, will have a hugely significant impact and outcome.

> 'Let every activity of your lives and every word that comes from your lips be marinated with the beauty of Jesus.' (Colossians 3: 17)